Praise for

A THOUSAND NAMES FOR JOY

"A genuine and fresh spiritual manifesto." —*Publishers Weekly*

"A thought-provoking commentary on the Tao Te Ching. Katie mirrors the openness that is characteristic of Lao-tzu's vision of reality."
—*Spirituality & Health*

"Byron Katie's teachings and everyday life are pure wisdom. *A Thousand Names for Joy* shows us the way to inner peace, and she directs us there fearlessly, relentlessly, and with utmost generosity. I have rarely seen anyone—spiritual teachers included—embody wisdom as powerfully as Katie in her passionate embrace of each and every moment."
—ROSHI BERNIE GLASSMAN, author of *Instructions to the Cook: A Zen Master's Lessons in Living a Life that Matters*

"A tribute to the awakened mind in action."
—*Sonoma Index-Tribune*

"*A Thousand Names for Joy* offers idiosyncratic and thought-provoking commentary on the chapters of the Tao Te Ching and its wonderful blend of practical tips and paradoxes."
—*Spirituality & Practice*

"Byron Katie is one of the truly great and inspiring teachers of our time. She has been enormously helpful to me personally. I love this very wise woman, and I encourage everyone to immerse themselves in this phenomenal book."
—DR. WAYNE W. DYER, author of *Inspiration*

"Expect to have cherished beliefs—perhaps the ones that are blocking happiness—challenged in a unique, honest way. And expect radically different perspectives on life and death, good and evil."

—*Common Ground*

"For those looking for daily inspiration, this is a book to keep by the bedside."

—*SRQ*

"Byron Katie's world is both amazing and curiously familiar. Her new book reveals what we have known all along—how large, spacious, and happy life can be. As you read *A Thousand Names for Joy*, you are immersed in that world, and pretty soon you are swimming—seeing the radiance that Katie sees."

—JOHN TARRANT,
author of *Bring Me the Rhinoceros and Other Zen Koans to Bring You Joy*

"Such joys as these may be hard to swallow at times, which is exactly why entering into Katie's process of inquiry may turn your life around. Her 'Way' of experiencing directly how we persist in imprisoning and harming ourselves by believing our mostly unexamined thoughts may be the deepest and most loving cognitive therapy of all."

—JON KABAT-ZINN,
author of *Coming to Our Senses: Healing Ourselves and the World Through Mindfulness*

BYRON KATIE

WITH STEPHEN MITCHELL

A
THOUSAND NAMES
FOR JOY

❋

Living in Harmony with the Way Things Are

 THREE RIVERS PRESS · NEW YORK

To you.

❊

Three Rivers Press and the Tugboat design are registered
trademarks of Random House, Inc.

Originally published in hardcover in the United States by
Harmony Books, New York, in 2007.

All epigraphs are quoted from *Tao Te Ching: A New English Version*
by Stephen Mitchell, copyright © 1988 by Stephen Mitchell,
reprinted by permission of HarperCollins Publishers.

Library of Congress Cataloging-in-Publication Data
Katie, Byron.
    A thousand names for joy : living in harmony with the way
things are / Byron Katie with Stephen Mitchell.
    1. Conduct of life.   2. Laozi. Dao de jing.   3. Tao.
4. Taoism.   I. Mitchell, Stephen, 1943–   II. Title.
BJ1571.K38   2007
170'.44—dc22   2006017754

ISBN 978-0-307-33924-9

Printed in the United States of America

DESIGN BY BARBARA STURMAN

10 9 8 7 6 5 4 3 2

First Paperback Edition

ALSO BY BYRON KATIE

I Need Your Love—Is That True?
(with Michael Katz)

Loving What Is
(with Stephen Mitchell)

CONTENTS

PREFACE

This book is a portrait of the awakened mind in action. It is also Byron Katie's response to the Tao Te Ching (pronounced *Dow De Jing*), the great Chinese classic that has been called the wisest book ever written.

Lao-tzu, the author of the Tao Te Ching, may have lived in the sixth century B.C.E., or he may be entirely legendary. I like to imagine him in frayed robes, an old man with a wispy beard, who spends much of his time in delighted silence, always available to people, serenely observing the infinite ways in which they make themselves unhappy. In many chapters of the Tao Te Ching, Lao-tzu describes himself through a figure called "the Master," the mature human being who has gone beyond wisdom and holiness to a world-including, world-redeeming sanity. There's nothing mystical or lofty about the Master. He (or she) is simply someone who knows the difference between reality and his thoughts about reality. He may be a mechanic or a fifth-grade teacher or the president of a bank or a homeless person on the streets. He is just like everyone else, except that he no longer believes that in this moment things should be different than they are. Therefore in all circumstances he remains at ease in the world, is efficient without the slightest effort, keeps his lightness of heart whatever happens, and, without intending to, acts with kindness toward himself and everyone else. He is who you are once you meet your mind with understanding.

A little about the author of this book. Byron Kathleen Reid (everyone calls her Katie) became severely depressed in her early thirties. She was a businesswoman and mother living in a little town in the high desert of southern California. For almost a decade she spiraled down into paranoia, rage, self-loathing, and constant thoughts of suicide; for the last two years she was often unable to leave her bedroom. Then, one morning in February 1986, out of nowhere, she experienced a life-changing realization. In the Buddhist and Hindu traditions there are various names for an experience like this. Katie calls it "waking up to reality." In that instant of no-time, she says,

> I discovered that when I believed my thoughts, I suffered, but that when I didn't believe them, I didn't suffer, and that this is true for every human being. Freedom is as simple as that. I found that suffering is optional. I found a joy within me that has never disappeared, not for a single moment. That joy is in everyone, always.

Soon afterward, rumors arose about a "lit lady" in Barstow, and people started seeking her out, asking how they could find the freedom that they saw shining in her. She became convinced that what they needed, if anything, was not her personal presence, but a way to discover for themselves what she had realized. Katie's method of self-inquiry, which she calls The Work, is an embodiment, in words, of the wordless questioning that had woken up in her on that February morning. It is a simple yet extremely powerful method and requires nothing more than a pen, paper, and an open mind. As reports spread about the remarkable transformations that people were experiencing through The Work, Katie was invited to present it publicly elsewhere in California, then throughout the United States, and eventually in Europe and across the world. She has been traveling for fifteen years now, sometimes nonstop, and has brought The Work to hundreds of thousands of people at free public events, in prisons, hospitals, churches, corporations, battered women's facilities, universities and schools, at weekend intensives, and at her nine-day School for The Work.

Katie doesn't know much about spiritual classics; in fact, before we met, she had never even heard of the Tao Te Ching. But she does know about joy and serenity, and she knows about the mind: how it can make us miserable, how we can use it to get free. So, from one point of view, Lao-tzu is a colleague, someone who has the same job, someone to have a conversation with, never mind that he's dead. This book is that very interesting conversation. Proceeding, like the Tao Te Ching, as variations on a theme, it expresses the same fundamental realization in many ways, under many circumstances.

Here's how the book came about. When I first met Katie, I was profoundly impressed by her openness of heart and her wisdom, which seemed to be a kind of transparence. She was a total innocent: she had read nothing, she knew nothing, about Buddhism or Taoism or any other spiritual tradition; she just had her own experience to refer to. The most wonderful insights would pop out of her mouth, sometimes straight from a sutra or an Upanishad, without any awareness on her part that anyone had ever said them before. Early in our marriage, partly out of curiosity, I began reading to her from the great spiritual teachers: Lao-tzu, the Buddha, the Zen masters, Spinoza, and others of that ilk. (She calls them "your dead friends.") Katie would take in their words, nodding sometimes, or saying, "That's accurate," or "Yes, it's exactly like that!" Occasionally, to my surprise, she would say, "That's true, as far as it goes, but it's a little 'off.' Here's how I'd say it."

Eventually I read her my version of the Tao Te Ching, all eighty-one chapters of it, and wrote down her responses, which were the raw material for this book. Sometimes, at my prompting, she would respond to every line; often she would focus on one passage, or elaborate on just a few lines. (The epigraphs that begin each of the following chapters quote the lines from the Tao Te Ching that are most relevant to what she is talking about.) Along the way, I would ask her to refine or expand upon something in the text, or I would point her in a particular direction that seemed helpful. Sometimes she had no reference for a question, and I felt as if I were asking a fish what it's like to live in water. I suggested the specifics for "beautiful" and "ugly" in chapter 2, for example, since I adore Mozart and I don't yet appreciate rap. It's useful that I have these strong likes and dislikes; it gives Katie a reference for concepts such as "noise," which are outside her experience of reality.

When we first began talking about the text, Katie asked me what *Tao* means. I told her that literally it means "the way," and that it's a word for ultimate reality, or, in her own terms, the way of it: what is. She was delighted. "But," she said, "I don't understand concepts like 'ultimate.' For me, reality is simple. There's nothing behind it or above it, and it holds no secrets. It's whatever is in front of you, whatever is happening. When you argue with it, you lose. It hurts not to be a lover of what is. I'm not a masochist anymore."

I have known the Tao Te Ching since 1973, and with particular intimacy since 1986, when I wrote my version. I respect it as much as any book in the world, I owe it a great deal, and I know its power. (A friend told me that when he was in emotional trouble as a young man, what saved him was that he read my version from cover to cover—notes included—every single day for a whole year.) It's wonderful to discover that there is such a thing as a manual on the art of living, a book this wise and this practical. But it is one thing to read about being in harmony with the way things are, or even to understand what that means, and quite another to actually live it. Even the wisest of books can't give us its wisdom. After we have read the profound insights and nodded our heads—"Stop trying to control," "Be completely present," "See the world as your self," "Let go," "Have faith in the way things are"—the central question remains: But how? *How* can we learn to do that?

Katie has written two books that show how to end suffering by questioning the thoughts that create it, the thoughts that argue with reality. No one knows how to let go, but anyone can learn exactly how to question a stressful thought. When you're feeling upset, for example, and it seems impossible to let go of that feeling, you can question the thoughts that say, "I'm not safe," "I can't do this," "She shouldn't have left me," "I'm too fat," "I need more money," "Life is unfair." After that questioning, you can't ever be the same. You may end up doing something or doing nothing, but however life unfolds, you'll be coming from a place of greater confidence and peace. And eventually, once your mind becomes clear, life begins to live itself through you, effortlessly, with the joy and kindness that Lao-tzu points us toward. Though reality itself is unnamable, Katie says, there are a thousand names for joy, because nothing is separate, and joy, deep down, is what we all are.

In the following chapters, when Katie uses the word *inquiry,* she specifically means The Work. The Work consists of four questions and what she calls a turnaround, which is a way of experiencing the opposite of what you believe. The questions are

1. Is it true?
2. Can you absolutely know that it's true?
3. How do you react when you believe that thought?
4. Who would you be without the thought?

When you first encounter them, these questions may seem merely intellectual. The only way to understand how they function is to use them yourself. But witnessing other people use them may give you a glimpse, even an experience, of their power. When they are answered honestly, they come alive; they mirror back truths that we can't see when we look outside. In the following pages you'll be able to read some extended examples of people applying The Work to their stressful thoughts, with Katie's lovingly incisive guidance. (You can find instructions on how to do The Work in the Appendix, and more detailed instructions on her website, www.thework.com, or in her book *Loving What Is*.)

The Work has been called self-help, but it is far more than that: it is self-realization, and it leads to the end of suffering. As we investigate a stressful thought, we see for ourselves that it's untrue; we get to look at the cause-and-effect of it, to observe in sobering detail exactly what modes of pain and confusion result from believing it; then we get a glimpse into the empty mirror, the world beyond our story of the world, and see what our life would be like without the thought; and finally we get to experience the opposite of what we have so firmly believed. Once we deeply question a thought, it loses its power to cause us pain, and eventually it ceases even to arise. "I don't let go of my thoughts," Katie says. "I meet them with understanding. Then *they* let go of *me*."

Questioning thoughts that seem to be true—thoughts that may even feel like part of our identity—takes courage, and in *A Thousand Names for Joy* Katie gives readers the powerful encouragement of seeing, in detail, the freedom that lives on the other side of inquiry. As you may have realized already, this book is more than a commentary on the Tao Te Ching. It is a glimpse into the depths of being, and into the life of a woman who for twenty years has been living what Lao-tzu wrote. The profound, lighthearted wisdom that it embodies is not theoretical; it is absolutely authentic. That is what makes the book so vivid and compelling. It's a portrait of a woman who is imperturbably joyous, whether she is dancing with her infant granddaughter or finds that her house has been emptied out by burglars, whether she stands before a man about to kill her or embarks on the adventure of walking to the kitchen, whether she learns that she is going blind, flunks a

"How Good a Lover Are You?" test, or is diagnosed with cancer. With its stories of total ease in all circumstances, it doesn't merely describe the awakened mind; it lets you see it, *feel* it, in action.

You may believe that although freedom was attainable thousands of years ago by a few enlightened masters, such a state is beyond the reach of anyone living in the modern world, and certainly beyond you. *A Thousand Names for Joy* has the power to change that belief.

—STEPHEN MITCHELL

NOTE: "Tao Te Ching" is shorthand for my book *Tao Te Ching: A New English Version*. You don't need to know anything about it in order to enjoy *A Thousand Names for Joy*. But even though this book is meant to be read as an independent text, each chapter relates to the corresponding chapter in my Tao Te Ching, and it's instructive to read them side by side.

A

THOUSAND NAMES

FOR JOY

INTRODUCTION

The Tao Te Ching is a wonderfully accurate description of the mind in harmony with the way things are. Ancient China, modern America—what does it matter? There's no time or space. When you don't believe your own thinking, life becomes effortless.

In my experience, confusion is the only suffering. Confusion is when you argue with what is. When you're perfectly clear, what is is what you want. So when you want something that's different from what is, you can know that you're very confused.

As you inquire into your own thoughts, you discover how attachment to a belief or story causes suffering. The mind's natural condition is peace. Then a thought enters, you believe it, and the peace seems to disappear. You notice the feeling of stress in the moment, and the feeling lets you know that you're opposing what is by believing the thought; it tells you that you're at war with reality. When you question the thought behind the feeling and realize that it isn't true, you become present outside your story. Then the story falls away in the light of awareness, and only the awareness of what really is remains. Peace is who you are without a story, until the next stressful

1

story appears. Eventually, inquiry becomes alive in you as the natural, wordless response of awareness to the thoughts that arise.

When the Tao Te Ching talks about "the Master," it is describing someone with a peaceful mind: a lover of what is. In this book I use the term *Master* because it's in the Tao Te Ching, and I use the pronoun "she" because all I can talk about is my own experience. But *Master* or *teacher* is not a word I normally use. It implies that we all don't teach equally. And that's not true. Everyone has equal wisdom. It is absolutely equally distributed. No one is wiser than anyone else. Ultimately, there's no one who can teach you except yourself.

I don't give advice. I know that everyone knows his own way, and I trust that. For forty-three years I was clueless, and then I found the way, or I was open enough for the way to find me. That's why I trust that you can find the way, too. No one is more special than another. There are no gurus who can magically enlighten you. But if a spiritual master is someone who has a happy life, who doesn't argue with reality, moves with every moment, effortlessly, delightedly, and loves it just as it is, then (if I existed anywhere) who knows, I may be a spiritual master.

I'm open to all that the mind brings, all that life brings. I have questioned my thinking, and I've discovered that it doesn't mean a thing. I shine internally with the joy of understanding. I know about suffering, and I know about joy, and I know who I am. Who I am is who you are, even before you have realized it. When there's no story, no past or future, nothing to worry about, nothing to do, nowhere to go, no one to be, it's all good.

1

The tao that can be told
is not the eternal Tao.

Y ou can't express reality in words. You limit it that way. You
squeeze it into nouns and verbs and adjectives, and the instant-
by-instant flow is cut off. The tao that can be told isn't the eternal
Tao, because trying to tell it brings it into time. It's stopped in time by
the very attempt to name it. Once anything is named, it's no longer
eternal. "Eternal" means free, without limit, without a position in
time or space, lived without obstacle.

There's no name for what's sitting in this chair right now. I am
the experience of the eternal. Even with the thought "God," it all
stops and manifests in time, and as I create "God," I have created
"not-God." You can substitute anything here—with the thought
"tree," I create "tree" and "not-tree"; the mechanism is the same. Before you name anything, the world has no things in it, no meaning.
There's nothing but peace in a wordless, questionless world. It's the
space where everything is already answered, in joyful silence.

In this world before words, there is only the real—undivided,
ungraspable, already present. Any apparently separate thing can't
be real, since the mind has created it with its names. When we understand this, the unreal becomes beautiful, because there's nothing
that can threaten the real. I don't ever see anything separate called

3

"tree" or "you" or "I." These things are only imagination, believed or unbelieved.

Naming is the origin of all the particular things that make up the world of illusion, the dream world. To break off part of the everything and name it "tree" is the first dream. I call it "first-generation thinking." Then thought begets thought, and we have "tall tree, beautiful tree, tree that I want to sit under, tree that would make good furniture, tree that I need to save," and the dream goes on and on. It takes a child just a moment to fall into the dream world, the dream of a world, when she first connects word with thing. And it takes you just a moment to question it, to break the spell and be grateful for the Tao of everything—tree, no tree; world, no world.

When the mind believes what it thinks, it names what cannot be named and tries to make it real through a name. It believes that its names are real, that there's a world out there separate from itself. That's an illusion. The whole world is projected. When you're shut down and frightened, the world seems hostile; when you love what is, everything in the world becomes the beloved. Inside and outside always match—they're reflections of each other. The world is the mirror image of your mind.

Not believing your own thoughts, you're free from the primal desire: the thought that reality should be different than it is. You realize the wordless, the unthinkable. You understand that any mystery is only what you yourself have created. In fact, there's no mystery. Everything is as clear as day. It's simple, because there really isn't anything. There's only the story appearing now. And not even that.

In the end, "mystery" is equal to "manifestations." You're just looking from a new perspective. The world is an optical illusion. It's just you, crazed and miserable, or you, delighted and at peace. In the end, "desire" is equal to "free from desire." Desire is a gift; it's about noticing. Everything happens *for* you, not *to* you.

I have questioned my thoughts, and I've seen that it's crazy to argue with what is. I don't ever want anything to happen except what's happening. For example, my ninety-year-old mother is dying of pancreatic cancer. I'm taking care of her, cooking and cleaning for her, sleeping beside her, living in her apartment twenty-three hours a day (my husband takes me out for a walk every morning). It has been a month now. It's as if her breath is the pulse of my life. I bathe her, I wash her in the most personal places, I medicate her, and I feel such a sense of gratitude. That's me over there, dying of cancer, spending my last few days sleeping and watching TV and talking, medicated with the most marvelous painkilling drugs. I am amazed at the beauty and intricacies of her body, my body. And the last day of her life, as I sit by her bedside, a shift takes place in her breathing, and I know: it's only a matter of minutes now. And then another shift takes place, and I know. Our eyes lock, and a few moments later she's gone. I look more deeply into the eyes that the mind has vacated, the mindless eyes, the eyes of the no-mind. I wait for a change to take place. I wait for the eyes to show me death, and nothing changes. She's as present as she ever was. I love my story about her. How else could she ever exist?

A man sticks a pistol into my stomach, pulls the hammer back, and says, "I'm going to kill you." I am shocked that he is taking his thoughts so seriously. To someone identified as an I, the thought of killing causes guilt that leads to a life of suffering, so I ask him, as kindly as I can, not to do it. I don't tell him that it's his suffering I'm thinking of. He says that he has to do it, and I understand; I remember believing that I had to do things in my old life. I thank him for doing the best he can, and I notice that I'm fascinated. Is this how she dies? Is this how the story ends? And as joy continues to fill me, I find it miraculous that the story is still going on. You can never know the ending, even as it ends. I am very moved at the sight of sky, clouds, and moonlit trees. I love that I don't miss one moment, one breath, of this amazing life. I wait. And wait. And in the end, he doesn't pull the trigger. He doesn't do that to himself.

What we call "bad" and what we call "good" both come from the same place. The Tao Te Ching says that the source of everything is called "darkness." What a beautiful name (if we must have a name)! Darkness is our source. In the end, it embraces everything. Its nature is love, and in our confusion we name it terror and ugliness, the unacceptable, the unbearable. All our stress results from what we imagine is in that darkness. We imagine darkness as separate from ourselves, and we project something terrible onto it. But in reality, the darkness is always benevolent.

What is the "darkness within darkness"? It's the mind that doesn't know a thing. This don't-know mind is the center of the universe—it *is* the universe—there's nothing outside it. The reason that darkness is the gateway to all understanding is that once the darkness is understood, you're clear that nothing is separate from you. No name, no thought, can possibly be true in an ultimate sense. It's all provisional; it's all changing. The dark, the nameless, the unthinkable—that is what you can absolutely trust. It doesn't change, and it's benevolent. When you realize this, you just have to laugh. There's nothing serious about life or death.

2

*When people see some things as good,
other things become bad.*

When they believe their thoughts, people divide reality into opposites. They think that only certain things are beautiful. But to a clear mind, everything in the world is beautiful in its own way.

Only by believing your own thoughts can you make the real unreal. If you don't separate reality into categories by naming it and believing that your names are real, how can you reject anything or believe that one thing is of less value than another? The mind's job is to prove that what it thinks is true, and it does that by judging and comparing this to that. What good is a this to the mind if it can't prove it with a that? Without proof, how can a this or a that exist?

For example, if you think that only Mozart is beautiful, there's no room in your world for rap. You're entitled to your opinion, of course, but other people think that rap is where it's at. How do you react when you believe that rap is ugly? You grit your teeth when you hear it, and when you have to listen (maybe you're a parent or a grandparent), you're in a torture chamber. I love that when mind is understood, there's room for rap as well as for Mozart. I don't hear anything as noise. To me, a car alarm is as beautiful as a bird singing. It's all the sound of God. By its very nature, the mind is infinite. Once it has questioned its beliefs, it can find beauty in all things; it's that open and free. This is not a philosophy. This is how the world really is.

If you believe that anyone's action is bad, how can you see the good in it? How can you see the good that comes out of it, maybe years later? If you see anyone as bad, how can you understand that we are all created equal? We're all teachers by the way we live. A blind drunk can teach more about why not to drink than an abstinent man in all his piety. No one has more or less goodness. No one who ever lived is a better or a worse human being than you.

A mind that doesn't question its judgments makes the world very small and dangerous. It must continue to fill the world with bad things and bad people, and in doing so it creates its own suffering. The worst thing that ever happened exists only in the past, which means that it doesn't exist at all. Right now, it's only a stressful thought in your mind.

Good things, bad things; good people, bad people. These opposites are valid only by contrast. Could it be that whatever seems bad to you is just something you haven't seen clearly enough yet? In reality—as it is in itself—every thing, every person, lies far beyond your capacity to judge.

Once you no longer believe your own thoughts, you act without doing anything, because there's no other possibility. You see that all thoughts of yourself as the doer are simply not true. I watch the hand that I call mine move toward the teacup. It has such intelligence, glides through the air so purposefully, arrives at the cup, fingers close around the handle, hand lifts cup, brings it to the lips, tilts it, tea flows into mouth, ahh. And all the time, no one is doing it. The doer is quite another, the one beyond the story of "I am."

Things seem to arise, and the Master lets them go because they're already gone. This apparent letting-go is not some saintly act of surrender. It's just that nothing ever belonged to her in the first place. How could she not let go of what doesn't exist except as the story of a past or a future?

She has only what she believes herself to have, so she has nothing, she needs nothing. She acts and waits for the miracle of what is, expecting nothing that would spoil the surprise. When her work is done, she forgets it, because there's nothing to remember. It's done. It's gone. She can't see what doesn't exist. Was her work good or bad? How ridiculous! Did it penetrate deeply or have no effect whatsoever? As if that were any of her business! Will it last forever? Did it last even for an instant?

3

Practice not-doing,
and everything will fall into place.

If you overesteem great men, you can't recognize the greatness within yourself. Any quality that you esteem in others is what *you* see, after all, and what you see comes from you. You undervalue yourself when you displace it and separate it from its origin. Admire Jesus' compassion or the Buddha's wisdom all you want, but what good can their qualities do you until you find them in yourself?

The mind is always looking for value. When it projects qualities away from itself, it robs itself of its own value. It starts traveling out of itself to find what it thinks it lacks, and its travels are endless, and it can never find its home.

The Master leads simply by being. "Being" looks like doing the dishes, answering the phone and the e-mail, shopping, going to work, driving the kids to school, feeding the dog, doing one thing at a time, without a past or future. She doesn't empty people's minds. She doesn't have to (even if that were possible). The way she helps people is by living out of don't-know, can't-know, no-need-to-know, not-possible-to-know, nothing-*to*-know. People are attracted to a life lived with such weightlessness, such lightness of heart. They begin to notice where they are, *who* they are, looking into the living mirror without their stressful thoughts.

I'm preparing a salad. I see flashes of colors. My hands begin to reach for what calls out to me. *Red!* and I reach for the beets. *Orange!* and I reach for the carrots. *Green!* and my hands move to the spinach. I feel the textures, I feel the dirt. *Purple!* and I move to the cabbage. All of life is in my hands. There's nothing lovelier than preparing a salad, its greens, reds, oranges, purples, crisp and juicy, rich as blood and fragrant as the earth. I move to the countertop. I begin to slice.

Just when I think that life is so good that it can't get any better, the phone rings and life gets better. I love that music. As I walk toward the phone, there's a knock at the door. Who could it be? I walk toward the door, filled with the given, the fragrance of the vegetables, the sound of the phone, and I have done nothing for any of it. I trip and fall. The floor is so unfailingly there. I experience its texture, its security, its lack of complaint. In fact, the opposite: it gives its entire self to me. I feel its coolness as I lie on it. Obviously it was time for a little rest. The floor accepts me unconditionally and holds me without impatience. As I get up, it doesn't say, "Come back, come back, you're deserting me, you owe me, you didn't thank me, you're ungrateful." No, it's just like me. It does its job. It is what it is. The fist knocks, the phone rings, the salad waits, the floor lets go of me—life is good.

Reality unfolds without desire, bringing with it more beauty, more luxury, more exquisite surprises than the imagination could ever devise. The mind, as it lives through its desires, demands that the body follow after it. How else can it mirror back original cause? Anger, sadness, or frustration lets us know that we're at war with the way of it. Even when we get what we wanted, we want it to last, and it doesn't, it can't. And because life is projected and mind is so full of confusion, there is no peace. But when you allow life to flow like water, you become that water. And you watch life lived to the ultimate, always giving you more than you need.

I wake up in the morning and see very little. I was able to see last night, but now it's all a blur, like seeing through a smogged-up window. (I was recently diagnosed with a degenerative condition of the cornea called Fuchs' dystrophy. There's no cure, and it has gotten a lot more intense over the past year.) I'm in a new hotel room, and I need to brush my teeth, shower, and pack. Where's the suitcase? And it comes to me; my hands know. The world is gray, but through the gray I can distinguish differences, and through these differences and the textures, I see everything I need to see in order to find my clothes. I feel my way to the bathroom, find the toothpaste and toothbrush, and squeeze the tube. Ooh! I've squeezed a huge gob of toothpaste onto the bristles, which brings a smile to my face: it seems that my teeth needed some extra help this morning. Then I step into the shower. It's tricky to understand the differences in bathroom fixtures, where the hot water is, which direction to turn the lever, how to convert the water from the spigot to the showerhead. Is the shower curtain tucked inside the tub so that the water won't run onto the floor? The lid to my bottle of soap is gone. Is it sitting on the ledge? Did it flush down the drain? Was the drain open or closed? I feel along the ridges of the tub for the lid. Do I have the right amount of shampoo in my hands? I'm sure it's fine, since not enough and too much are always the perfect amount. The water is hot. This is working. I'm so grateful as I step out of the shower onto the . . . is it my robe or the bath mat?

Makeup is interesting. I use three items only: one for eyes, one for cheeks, one for lips. I do my best with the woman thing, it feels right, it's over, for better or worse. This face is the way of it. It's prepared. It will do its job. "Sweetheart, do these things go together? Is this top brown or black or blue?" Through Stephen's eyes, my clothes seem to be coordinated, and that works for me. I have an interview. I'm glad he can show me the way, beyond what he can know. Without words, through his actions, I know where the doorknobs are, where the stairs are, where the path is. Eventually, in the afternoon, my eyes begin to clear up, and *they* begin to show me the way. I love how it all works. I love how the mornings prepare me for life, and how my afternoon vision gives me glimpses into what was only imagined in the first place.

4

It is like the eternal void:
filled with infinite possibilities.

We can call the Tao "reality." We can also call it "mind." Mind is a natural resource that never comes to an end. When it no longer believes its thoughts, it has entered the dimension of the unlimited. It's like a bottomless well: you can always draw from it, and it will always give you the water of life. Because it is completely open and sees that nothing is true, it is filled with more possibilities than we can ever imagine.

Lao-tzu says, "I don't know who gave birth to it." I do. *You* give birth to it every time your own mind opens to what is beyond what you think you know. And when your mind opens, what is beyond knowing, what is older than "God," streams in as a gift. There is no end to that gift.

5

The Tao doesn't take sides;
it gives birth to both good and evil.

The darkness, the void, the space that the mind is terrified to enter, is the beginning of all life. It's the womb of being. Fall in love with it, and when you do, it will immediately be taken from you, as you witness the birth of light. The Tao doesn't take sides. It embraces both the darkness and the light. They're equal.

The Master *can't* take sides. She's in love with reality, and reality includes everything—both sides of everything. Her arms are open to it all. She finds everything in herself: all crimes, all holiness. She doesn't see saints as saints or sinners as sinners; they're just people who are suffering or not, believing their thoughts or not. She doesn't see any difference between states of consciousness. What's called bliss and what's called ordinary mind are equal; one is not a higher state than the other. There's nothing to strive for, nothing to leave behind. There's only one, and not even that. It doesn't matter how you attempt to be disconnected, that's not a possibility. Believing a stressful thought is an attempt to break the connection. That's why it feels so uncomfortable.

All suffering is mental. It has nothing to do with the body or with a person's circumstances. You can be in great pain without any suffering at all. How do you know you're supposed to be in pain? Because

14

that's what's happening. To live without a stressful story, to be a lover of what is, even in pain—that's heaven. To be in pain and believe that you shouldn't be in pain—that's hell. Pain is actually a friend. It's nothing I want to get rid of, if I can't. It's a sweet visitor; it can stay as long as it wants to. (And that doesn't mean I won't take a Tylenol.)

Even pain is projected: it's always on its way out. Can your body hurt when you're not conscious? When you're in pain and the phone rings and it's the call you've been waiting for, you mentally focus on the phone call, and there's no pain. If your thinking changes, the pain changes.

I have an Israeli friend who is paralyzed from his neck to his toes. He used to see himself as a victim, and he had all the proof—the mind is good at that. He was certain that life was unfair. But after doing The Work for a while, he came to realize that reality is just the way it should be. He doesn't have a problem now. He's a happy man in a paralyzed body. And he didn't do anything to change his mind. He simply questioned his thinking, and mind changed.

The same kind of freedom can happen to people who have lost their husbands or wives or children. An unquestioned mind is the only world of suffering. I was once doing The Work with some maximum-security prisoners in San Quentin, men who had been given life sentences for murder, rape, and other violent crimes. I asked them to begin by writing down their angry or resentful thoughts: "I am angry at _____ because _____." And then I asked each of them in turn to read the first sentence he had written. One man was shaking with rage so uncontrollably that he couldn't finish reading his sentence, which was "I am angry at my wife because she set fire to our apartment and my little girl was burned to death." For years he had been living in the hell of his anger, loss, and despair. But he was an unusual man, who really wanted to know the truth. Later in the session, after he read another statement he had written—"I need my daughter to be alive"—I asked him The Work's second question: "Can you absolutely know that that's true?" He went inside himself for the answer, and it blew his mind. He said, "No, I can't absolutely know that." I said, "Are you breathing?" He said, "Yes," and his face lit up. And eventually he discovered that he *didn't* need his daughter to be alive, that beneath all his rage and despair he was doing just fine, and that he couldn't even absolutely know what the best thing for his daughter was. The tears and laughter that poured out of him were the most moving things in the world. It was a great privilege to be sitting with this amazing man. And all he had done was question his own beliefs.

6

Empty yet inexhaustible,
it gives birth to infinite worlds.

Mind gives birth to infinite worlds—of this and that, loss and sorrow, good and evil. It's complete from the beginning, and yet it's inexhaustible in the production of what isn't. Believing what you think, you're carried off into the endless dramas of the self.

Until there's peace within you, there is no peace in the world, because you are the world, you are the earth. The story of earth is all there is of earth and beyond. When you're in dreamless sleep at night, is there a world? Not until you wake up and say, "I." When the I arises, welcome to the movie of who you think you are. But if you question it, there's no attachment, it's just a great movie. Get the popcorn: here it comes!

I live in completeness. All of us do, though we may not realize it. I don't know anything; I don't have to figure anything out. I gave up forty-three years of thinking that went nowhere, and now I exist as a don't-know mind. This leaves nothing but peace and joy in my life. It's the absolute fulfillment of watching everything unfold in front of me as me.

7

It was never born;
thus it can never die.

What is death? How can you die? Who says that you were ever
born? There is only the life of an unquestioned thought. There
is only mind, if anything. After you think the thought "I'm going to
die," where did that thought go? Isn't another thought your only
proof that it's true? Who would you be without your story? That's
how the world begins. "I." "I am." "I am a woman." "I am a woman
who is getting up to brush her teeth and go to work." And on and on,
until the world becomes denser and denser. "I am"—question that.
That is where the world ends, until what's left comes back to explore
the next concept. Do you continue after death? If you question your
mind deeply enough, you'll see that what you are is beyond life and
death.

The questioned mind, because it's no longer seeking, is free to
travel limitlessly. It understands that since it was never born, it can
never die. It's infinite, because it has no desires for itself. It withholds
nothing. It's unconditional, unceasing, fearless, tireless, without reser-
vations. It has to give. That's its nature. Since all beings are its own
dear reflected self, it's always receiving, giving itself back to itself.

A stuck mind is the only death—death by torture. The unquestioned mind, believing what it thinks, lives in dead ends—frustrated,

hopeless, forever trying to find a way out, only to experience another dead end. And each time the problem is solved, another problem pops up. That's how the unquestioned mind has to live. It's stuck in the oldest stories, like a dinosaur still chewing on the same old grass.

When I woke up to reality in 1986, I noticed stories arising inside me that had been troubling mankind forever. I felt absolutely committed to undoing every stressful story that had ever been told. I was the mind of the world, and each time one of the stories was seen for what it really was and thus undone in me, it was undone in the whole world, because there is only one thinker.

The Master stays behind, in the student's position, always watching, noticing, experiencing, realizing, and enveloped in reality, in the way of it. That's how she stays ahead of any problem. There's nothing wasted, nothing unabsorbed. She wouldn't leave anything out.

She is detached from all things in the sense that when they come, that's what she wants, and when they go, that's what she wants. It's all fine with her. She is in love with it as it comes and goes. She is one with it all. The branch sways in the breeze; as she watches, she sees that it's not true, and in that lack of separation, she becomes the branch in the breeze. She hears the sound of the garbage truck, she becomes the sound, and she tingles with gratitude that she is that. What self is there to let go of? The world begins with her, and it ends with her, right now.

8

The supreme good is like water,
which nourishes all things without trying to.
It is content with the low places that people disdain.

Clear mind, the supreme good, is like water. It is transparent, it sparkles, it flows everywhere without obstruction. It is beautiful and profound, the nourishment that feeds all things internally, without trying to.

A clear mind is by its very nature in a place of humility. It loves the low places. It prefers being in the audience to being on stage (though when people put it in the spotlight, it loves that, too). It lives at the feet of everything else, because it *is* everything else. In its gratitude at being everything beautiful, it bows at the feet of the master we call stone, bush, beggar, ant, grass. It finds itself as the bird soaring overhead and doesn't know how to fly and notices that it's flying anyway.

When the mind is clear, life becomes very simple. I have the thought to stand up and do the dishes. I notice a sense of profound excitement as the body rises with this thought. How childlike it is as it moves to the kitchen, to the sink. I turn the handle, experience the water on my hands, pour some liquid soap onto a sponge. Amazing. It's not ever about doing the dishes, until I hold one and see it change from crusted or sticky to wet and soapy, to shiny, to dry, so that it can serve again. Everything changes. I never know what anything is going to be. Without believing any thought of a future, there's no way of knowing what is me and what is the plate, the soap, the water, the world of bubbles and shine.

The clear mind, loving the music of itself as it moves from chair to sink, notices that even though what's left of thoughts is ravishingly beautiful, it also isn't true. It's the music, the sound track, meaningless forever, as life appears to happen. Who would wage war against a sound track? What craziness could oppose such simplicity? The last judgment: body rises and moves to sink, soap, water, shine. It's a beautiful story. It's all there is to life. It is the only life.

I'm happy to be this sixty-three-year-old woman. I love that I weigh 160 pounds, I love that I'm not any smarter than I am, I love that my skin is getting wrinkled and loose, I love that some mornings I'm almost blind and there's just a haze of world and I can barely see where I'm going. I love where my hands have been put, and I love how I am breathed and positioned and angled. I love what I see now as I look out the window, one solid picture: trees, sky, lawn, brick chimney, bougainvillea, HOUSE FOR SALE sign, hedge, canal, ducks, and I can't separate one from the other. I love it that as I walk upstairs my steps are not too fast, not too slow, not too far apart, I love how in their own wisdom my feet step on the perfect portion of floor, in exactly the right rhythm. How miraculous their movement is! My hand reaches out to the banister on the staircase, its support, without thought or reason. And again the footsteps, the hand moves, the head looks up: a rainbow on my wall. Nothing could be better than this moment.

Why would I be you or someone else when we all can walk up a staircase, we all can stand and move in our own way? No one has more or less opportunity to be himself, to love and be content with himself. Why would I compare or compete? Comparing is nothing more than believing the story that a past would invent as a future. It's so much simpler to be what I am. (As if I could be anything else.)

9

Do your work, then step back.
The only path to serenity.

There's a natural balance in things. If you go too far to one ex-treme, life kindly brings you back toward the center. What goes up must come down, and what comes down must go up. Up and down are different aspects of the same thing.

So are inside and outside. Most people think that the world is outside them. They live life backward, running after security and approval, as if by making enough money or getting enough praise they could be happy once and for all. But nothing outside us can give us what we're really looking for.

I do my work and don't even need to step back from it, because it never belonged to me in the first place. Nothing belongs to me. Everything comes and goes. Serenity is an open door.

10

*Can you coax your mind from its wandering
and keep to the original oneness?*

When you don't believe your thoughts, what is is what you are.
There's no separation in it. You're everything. Only the unquestioned mind would believe that you're an I living inside a body.

What is the original oneness? Chair-hand-cup-window-sky, before "chair," "hand," "cup," "window," "sky." You don't need to return to it, since you've never left. How could you leave it? Where else is there to go? The center of the universe is wherever you are, and it's everywhere. It's the origin and the end point, the beauty of darkness, the exultation of nothing. And only the center is real. When you understand that, you realize that even oneness is unnecessary.

It's like falling in love with yourself. There's nothing to do, no one to be, no responsibility, no meaning, no suffering, no death. You no longer believe yourself into a separate, distant polarity, where you're identified as a tiny speck making grandiose efforts to prove that something is true. Realizing that you've never left the original oneness means that you were never born and you can never die.

What suppleness this realization allows! You're immune to anything the mind would superimpose onto reality: any disappointment or sorrow. If I lose all my money, good. If I get cancer, good. If my husband leaves me, good. If my husband stays, that's good, too. Who wouldn't always say yes to reality if that's what you're in love with? What can happen that I wouldn't welcome with all my heart?

I don't know what's best for me or you or the world. I don't try to impose my will on you or on anyone else. I don't want to change you or improve you or convert you or help you or heal you. I just welcome things as they come and go. That's true love. The best way of leading people is to let them find their own way.

One day, a few years after I first found The Work inside me, my sons began to fight in our living room. I was sitting on the couch, very close to them. They were two grown men, in their twenties, and here they were on the floor, wrestling and pummeling each other and yelling, "Mom, Mom, make him stop!" All I saw were two men trying to connect, not knowing another way. I sat there just watching them, just loving them, and in that moment I didn't have the slightest thought of intervening. There was no doing, no trickery to it. And suddenly they noticed, and they stopped fighting. I loved that they found their own solution. That was the last time they ever fought.

11

We work with being,
but non-being is what we use.

As the mind realizes itself, it stops identifying with its own thoughts. This leaves a lot of open space. A mature mind can entertain any idea; it is never threatened by opposition or conflict, because it knows that it can't be hindered. When it has no position to defend or identity to protect, it can go anywhere. There's never anything to lose, because there's no thing that exists in the first place. Laughter pours out of it, and tears of gratitude, from the experience of its own nature.

Everything appears to come into me. I watch and witness what comes out of me. I'm the center of everything. I hear opinions and concepts, and because there's no I to identify as, I take it all in as being, and everything that comes out of the experience has been bathed in non-being, has been deleted and put out again. It comes in, it synthesizes, it's deleted, and what goes out is non-being appearing as being. When you realize that you're no one, you're comfortable with everyone, no matter how desperate or depraved they may seem. There's no suffering I can't enter, knowing that it's already resolved, knowing that it's always myself I'm meeting.

As we question what we believe, we come to see that we're not who we thought we were. The transformation comes out of the infinite polarity of mind, which we've rarely experienced, because the I-know mind has been so much in control. And as we inquire, our world changes, because we're working with the projector—mind—and not with what is projected. We lose our entire world, the world as we understood it. And each time we inquire, reality becomes kinder.

The part that is doing the questioning is the neutral part of the mind, the center, which can take one polarity of mind to the other. This neutral part offers the confused, stuck, I-know polarity the option to open itself to the polarity of mind that holds the sane, clear, loving answers that make sense to the I-know mind. The neutral part doesn't have a motive or desire, a *should* or a *shouldn't;* it's a bridge for this polarity to cross over. And as the I-know mind is educated, it dissolves into the polarity of wisdom. What's left is absolutely sane, undivided, and free. Of course, all this is just a metaphor, since there is only one mind. The bottom line is that when the mind is closed, the heart is closed; when the mind is open, the heart is open. So if you want to open your heart, question your thinking.

Inquiry always leaves you with less of a story. Who would you be without your story? You never know until you inquire. There is no story that is you or that leads to you. Every story leads away from you. You are what exists before all stories. You are what remains when the story is understood.

Life on the other side of inquiry is so simple and obvious that it can't be imagined beforehand. Everything is seen to be perfect, just the way it is. Hope and faith aren't needed in this place. Earth turned out to be the heaven I was longing for. There's such abundance here, now, always. There's a table. There's a floor. There's a rug on the floor. There's a window. There's a sky. A sky! I could go on and on celebrating the world I live in. It would take a lifetime to describe this moment, this now, which doesn't even exist except as my story. And isn't it fine? The wonderful thing about knowing who you are is that you're always in a state of grace, a state of gratitude for the abundance of the apparent world. I overflow with the splendor, the generosity of it all. And I didn't do anything for it but notice.

The litmus test for self-realization is a constant state of gratitude. This gratitude is not something you can look for or find. It comes from another direction, and it takes you over completely. It's so vast that it can't be dimmed or overlaid. The short version would be "mind in love with itself." It's the total acceptance and consumption of itself reflected back at the same moment in the central place that is like fusion. When you live your life from that place of gratitude, you've come home.

12

The Master observes the world
but trusts her inner vision.

The Master observes the colors of the world, its sounds, flavors, and thoughts. Since they are all reflections of mind and her realization of that is precise and indisputable, she is never fooled. What has no beginning can't have an end. She understands that what is unfathomably good gives birth to it all. That's what she trusts. There is no inside or outside. It's all appearing in the delighted eternity of her own mind.

She watches things as they come and go. The *nature* of things is to come and go, with or without her permission, so why not enjoy the show? It's all so beautiful. Without something, what fun is it to be nothing?

13

Love the world as your self;
then you can care for all things.

When you're a lover of what is, it's obvious that the world is your own face in the mirror. But *how* do you become a lover of what is? The "how" has been a mystery till now. Now it's clear that all you need to do is investigate your stressful thoughts. The four questions and turnaround of The Work will take you as deep as you want to go.

People think that they need to get "enlightened" in order to be free, and nobody knows what enlightenment is. Yes, it's in the sacred texts, and yes, this guru or that lama says he has attained it, but that's just a concept; it's the story of a past. The truth is that there's no such thing as enlightenment. No one is permanently enlightened; that would be the story of a future. There's only enlightenment in the moment. Do you believe a stressful thought? Then you're confused. Do you realize that the thought isn't true? Then you're enlightened to it. It's as simple as that. And then the next thought comes, and maybe you're enlightened to it as well, and maybe not.

I have found that there are no new stressful thoughts, they're all recycled. People try to "let go" of their thoughts. That's like telling your child you don't want her and kicking her out onto the street. I used to go out into the desert to get away from the world, and I took the whole world with me in my head—every concept that had ever been experienced. I was undoing the thoughts that run through the mind of every human being. Thoughts are no more individual than the TV program that everyone watches. I have found that all over the world, in every language and culture, people suffer because they believe the same stressful thoughts: "My mother doesn't love me." "I'm not good enough." "I'm fat." "I need more money." "My husband should understand me." "My wife shouldn't have left me." "The world needs to be saved." Of course, I would never ask people not to believe their thoughts. Not only would that be unkind; it isn't *possible* for people not to believe what they believe. We can't help believing our thoughts until we question them. That's the way of it.

People used to ask me if I was enlightened, and I would say, "I don't know anything about that. I'm just someone who knows the difference between what hurts and what doesn't." I am someone who wants only what is. To meet as a friend each concept that arose turned out to be my freedom.

THE WORK IN ACTION

Dyslexia

NOTE: This dialogue, and the other three that follow, took place before an audience of about 350 people. Each man or woman sitting opposite Katie on the stage had written out a Judge-Your-Neighbor Worksheet; the instructions were: "Fill in the blanks below, writing about someone you haven't yet forgiven 100 percent. Do not write about yourself yet. Use short, simple sentences. Please don't censor yourself—allow yourself to be as judgmental and petty as you really feel. Don't try to be 'spiritual' or kind." In Katie's responses, the four questions and invitation to the turnaround are printed in boldface. (For a copy of the Worksheet and instructions on how to do The Work, see the Appendix, page 265.)

A first experience of The Work, as a reader or an onlooker, can be unsettling. Katie's deep compassion, which is totally without pity because she sees everyone as free, can seem harsh to those who are used to pitying others and themselves. "I am your heart," Katie has said. "If you invite me in, I am the depth you haven't listened to. It had to get louder, to appear as me, because your beliefs were blocking it out. I am you on the other side of inquiry. I am the voice so covered up with beliefs that you can't hear it on the inside. So I appear out here, in your face—which is really inside yourself." It helps to remember that all the participants—Katie, the person doing The Work with her, and the audience—are on the same side here; all of them are looking for the truth. If Katie ever seems to be insensitive toward someone, you'll realize, upon closer examination, that she's making fun of the thought that is causing the suffering, never of the person who is suffering.

You'll notice that Katie is very free in her use of terms of endearment. This annoys some people (not all of them New Yorkers); one reader of *Loving What Is* grumbled that if she wanted to hear a woman calling everyone "sweetheart" or "honey," she would go to a truck stop in Oklahoma. To her, these endearments sounded conventional and insincere; for Katie, they are the literal truth. Everyone she meets is the beloved.   —S.M.

PETER [handing Katie a Worksheet]: Katie, I'm dyslexic, so I had someone read me the questions and I dictated the answers to him. Can I give you my Worksheet and you can read what I said?

KATIE: Sure. [Reading from Peter's Worksheet] *I'm angry at my reading and writing disability, my dyslexia, because it makes it hard to write, read, communicate, do the Internet, e-mail, work.*

PETER: In today's world.

KATIE: Yes. So "You need to read and write"—**is that true?**

PETER: Only to communicate with somebody who's not in the present location.

KATIE: "You need to read and write" at all, even for that reason—**is it true?**

PETER [after a pause]: No. Ultimately, it's not.

KATIE: How old are you?

PETER: Forty-three.

KATIE: You've been okay for forty-three years.

PETER: I don't know if I'd use the word *okay*.

KATIE: Well, other than your thinking, how's your body?

PETER: My body's great.

KATIE: Except for your thoughts, haven't you done well?

PETER: Yes. But I've had all the education possible to try to teach me how to read and write . . .

KATIE: "You need to read and write"—**is that true?**

PETER: No. I actually do pretty well without it.

KATIE: Good to know. Feel that, sweetheart. For forty-three years, other than your thinking, you've done fine! Your boots match.

PETER: Actually, I made them. [The audience applauds and hoots.]

KATIE: People who read and write may have a problem with that. [The audience laughs.]

PETER: I know.

KATIE: We're too busy reading and writing. [The audience laughs.]

PETER: The thing is, my mind doesn't work in two dimensions, it works in three dimensions.

KATIE: **How do you react when you believe the thought** "I need to read and write," and you can't, because you're dyslexic?

PETER [with tears in his eyes]: Ashamed. Embarrassed. Society takes reading and writing for granted. It hurts.

KATIE: Give me a peaceful reason to believe that you need to read and write. Or to read *or* write.

PETER: It would be nice to be able to help my ten-year-old son with his homework.

KATIE: Oh, really? You've been spared! [The audience laughs.]

PETER: You're right.

KATIE: It's like you're wishing for an additional job. And the reality of it leaves him with something very important; it leaves him responsible for what he learns. That way he really learns. Anyway, that's not a *peaceful* reason; that one upsets you. It brings you to tears. Give me a peaceful reason to believe that you need to read and write.

PETER [after a long pause]: There isn't a peaceful reason.

KATIE: So why would you believe it? It's not true that you need to read and write, I hear from you. You've been fine for forty-three years. You don't need to learn to read and write to be fine and talented, or to be a good father. Give me a peaceful reason to believe that you need to read and write. There must be some good reason . . .

PETER: There is no peaceful reason to keep the thought.

KATIE: So what I'm hearing is that you only believe "I need to read and write" as a way to suffer.

PETER: That's true.

KATIE: So if you want to suffer, believe that lie. "I need to read and write"—**turn it around.** What's the opposite of "I need to read and write"?

PETER: I don't need to read and write. I don't need to read and write any more than I'm already capable of doing to survive.

KATIE: Yes. Welcome to the truth. Now give me three reasons why your life is better because you don't read and write.

PETER: Hmm. Well, I don't read a newspaper, so I don't have to listen to all that bullshit every day. [The audience applauds.] I use my imagination and my artistic skills for entertainment or pleasure.

KATIE: That's two. Why is your life better because you don't read and write?

PETER: It frees up a lot of time.

KATIE: A *lot* of time.

PETER: It allows me to not get involved in politics and all the day-to-day happenings of life that stress people out, I guess. So, yes, my life is better in that way because . . . it's not something I need to do. I can hire people to have that stress for me.

KATIE: You can hire people to read and write for you. Or you can just ask us.

PETER: Right.

KATIE: You asked *me* to read your Worksheet. *I* said yes.

PETER: Right. I've had people call me at my office to make an appointment, and . . .

KATIE: Your office? How is it possible to have an office if you can't read and write?

PETER: Umm . . . I just do.

KATIE: So, sweetheart, other people can do your reading and writing *for* you, it frees you up to do other things, it frees you to let your creative energies flow. It gives you a lot of free time.

PETER: But it's humiliating when I ask somebody how to spell something and they say, "What are you, stupid?"

KATIE: Well, what's your answer to that?

PETER: "No."

KATIE: There you have it! [The audience laughs.] Do you have a problem with the word *no*? Do you have a problem with the truth?

PETER: I'm beginning to like it much more.

KATIE: So, sweetheart, you be the mean world, the people who say, "What are you, stupid?" Be that world. I'm going to be a kind, honest, clear, dyslexic man; I'm going to be you. Okay?

PETER: Okay.

KATIE: "Hi . . . would you read this for me?"

PETER: "What's your problem; can't you read it yourself?"

KATIE: "Actually, I can't. I'm dyslexic."

PETER: "What's dyslexia?"

KATIE: "Well, I'm glad you asked. I don't have the ability to read. I see things backward or reversed. Words just don't make sense to me. It has to do with the way my brain sees things, and I just can't read. I've tried everything, people have tried to teach me, and it doesn't work, because of the way my brain is wired."

PETER: "You must be a fucking moron."

KATIE: "Well, you know, actually my IQ is pretty high. Would you read this for me?"

PETER: "No, I won't read it. That's your fucking problem."

KATIE: "Okay. Thank you." And then I go ask someone else. And I don't bother to tell him it's *not* a problem, that I don't want the *wrong* person reading for me. And he shows me who's not supposed to read to me. He eliminated himself perfectly. You don't want the wrong person reading to you, after all. Someone like that might mess with the words, who knows? So "You're disabled"—**is that true?** If you had to say at this point if the dyslexia is a gift or a disability, *honestly*, what would you say?

PETER [crying]: I've always thought of it as a horrible disability. But now, for the first time, I'm getting a glimpse of something else.

KATIE: No one but another dyslexic knows the hell that you've been through. How people have shoved you and insulted you and seen you as stubborn and stupid rather than dyslexic. And you, trying to pull out of your hat an ability that you don't have. That's hell.

PETER [crying]: It *has* given me so many gifts, but sometimes the bad just overwhelms you, and you can't see the good.

KATIE: And the punishment, over and over, and then the fear that someone will find out.

PETER: Yes, it was the punishment that I was put through in school, the punishment I put myself through as an adult.

KATIE: Teachers putting you up in front of the class, to do what you couldn't do.

PETER: They'd say, "Why don't you read this chapter in front of the class?" It made me feel about this big [putting his thumb and index finger close together].

KATIE: Because you believed that you were supposed to be able to read, and that there was something wrong with you.

PETER: Yes. Well, society takes it for granted.

KATIE: Who took it for granted? **Turn it around**—that would be you, angel. So if you had to say, at this point, if it's a gift or a disability . . . What would you say the truth is—not wishful thinking, but simply the truth? Is it a disability or a gift?

PETER: It's becoming more of a gift.

KATIE: I love that you catch up with that. You've been experiencing something very, very beautiful.

PETER: It's taken me a long time.

KATIE: It saves you a lot of time. It *totally* frees you up. You get to do what everyone wants to do: have time. It's a wonderful thing. People can read huge long documents and just give you the short version.

PETER: Right. That's exactly what I do.

KATIE: "You're disabled"—**is that true?**

PETER: I feel like it some days.

KATIE: So I'm asking you right now. "You're disabled"—**is that true?** "Not to be able to read and write is a disability"—**is that true?** I'm not talking about the way the world sees it.

PETER: Okay, if you're not talking about the way the world sees it, then no.

KATIE: *Feel* that! The world would tell you a lot of things, and you know how far that goes.

PETER: I know, but when you're standing on the checkout line at the supermarket, and you can't write a check, and the lady behind you is saying, "Would you hurry up?" And you start shaking . . .

KATIE: Well, what's the answer?

PETER: Use a credit card! [Peter, Katie, and the audience laugh.]

KATIE: "You're disabled"—**is that true?**

PETER [smiling]: No, I'm not! [More laughter.] No, I'm far from disabled. I'm an extremely talented person.

KATIE: Yes. So what would you choose—that, or the ability to read and write? If you *had* to make a choice?

PETER: That's a tough question. My little brother is a molecular geneticist.

KATIE: You've been spared again! [The audience laughs.]

PETER: I've been spared again? Yes. But he did find the gene for osteoporosis.

KATIE: So, if you *had* to make the choice between being able to read and what you've got . . .

PETER: I've had days where I would have cut my right hand off to be able to read.

KATIE: Well, those were the days! [The audience laughs.] And I'm asking you *now*, right now. This is where it counts. This is the only place where life counts. Right here, right now, if you had to choose between what you've got and the ability to read and write. I'm talking about your talents, your intelligence . . . everything you are.

PETER: No. I wouldn't trade it.

KATIE: So sit in that for a moment. [Long pause.] Don't you love you the way you are!

PETER: Yes, I do.

KATIE: Well, I do too.

PETER: Thank you.

KATIE: You know those people I was describing to you, the ones who didn't understand, who were so impatient? I was one of those. That's how I treated my daughter. She's dyslexic.

PETER: You bitch! [The audience laughs.]

KATIE [nodding her head]: Yes. [Pause.] You know what a bitch is? Someone who simply believes what she thinks. Pure ignorance! That leaves *you* to love us, until we understand. But only if you want to be happy.

PETER [with tears in his eyes]: Thank you.

KATIE: You're welcome. [Pause.] I would sit with my daughter day after day, drilling her on her reading, over and over, until often she was in tears. Her teachers told me that's what I needed to drill her on, and I believed them.

PETER: Yes, I went through the same thing. My brothers are outside playing, and I'm stuck at the table—it felt like I was strapped to it with duct tape, and . . . "You have to do this or you can't do anything else."

KATIE: And that left you to do nothing else but spin your thoughts. And feeling like you're missing something, like there's something lacking, and all the time it's a gift! That's asleepness. That's as asleep as I was as the mother of a dyslexic. My daughter was asleep—she thought she should be able to read, too! And she couldn't. So *she* believed it, *I* believed it; we were both disabled. And then we began to question our minds. She's *so* smart. When I need help, I go to her. She's *so* amazing. She sees things that I can't begin to see.

PETER: Yes. We can. We can.

KATIE: Thank goodness for dyslexics in the world. And if you get over yourself, we all benefit. And the way you get over yourself is to start questioning what we taught you to believe. The truth can only be found inside you. So [reading from Peter's Worksheet] *I'm angry at my reading and writing disability, my dyslexia, because it makes it hard to write, read, communicate, do the Internet, e-mail, work.*

PETER: Yes, it makes it hard to read and write.

KATIE: Yes, when you can't, it's hard. [The audience laughs.]

PETER: It's like running up a hill that you can never reach the top of.

KATIE: Well, yeah! But only for forty-three years. So that's not your thing. People say, "Can't you write a check?" "No." Or if you can do that much, "Can't you hurry?" The answer is "No . . . I can't. I'm dyslexic." They're just asking for the truth. And if *you're* not going to educate us, who is? "I'm dyslexic . . . I can't. That ability belongs to you, not me. Will you help me with this check?"

PETER: It's amazing how many ways I've learned how to compensate. My checkbook. [He hands it to Katie.]

KATIE [looking at the checkbook]: Oh, I love that! I love that! [To the audience] He's got the numbers from one to a thousand spelled out. So he can copy them, copy how it's spelled. So it's "one, two, three, four, five, six . . . ten, twenty, thirty, forty . . .

sixteen, seventeen, hundred thousand" . . . Any of you dyslexics, talk to Peter; he's got it down here. I mean, it's not one to a thousand, there are three rows plus two. It's all right there. It's brilliant. It's amazing, I'd have to write from one to a thousand, that's my handicap. I'd have to write the whole thing!

PETER: Well, writing a Worksheet I find very difficult, because when I *do* write it, it is all phonetically, and if I have a thought, I have to stop and think how to spell the word, and I lose my thought, so it interrupts the ability to be fluent within trying to fill out a Worksheet. And that's why I had somebody write out this Worksheet for me. And also so that it would be legible.

KATIE: You know, what's really cool is when you ask your son to do it for you. That gives him a lot. And it certainly gives you a lot. So you ask someone to write it out for you, or you use a tape recorder.

PETER: I've been playing with that for a little while.

KATIE: Good. The main thing is to capture the concept that you're believing. It doesn't have to be a whole Worksheet. If you have the thought "I'm handicapped," just hold that. Notice how everything you think will try to play off that for a while, and then just hold it. And then, begin to question it. So [reading from Peter's Worksheet] *It makes it hard to write, read, communicate, do the Internet, e-mail, work.* "It's hard for you to do the Internet, e-mail, and work"—**is that true?**

PETER: Yes.

KATIE: Do you get other people to do it for you?

PETER: Yes, my ten-year-old son.

KATIE: "It's hard for you to communicate, do the Internet, e-mail, and work"—**is that true?**

PETER: Yes. When there's no one around.

KATIE: When there *are* people around, is it hard?

PETER: Um . . . no.

KATIE: Okay. So *sometimes* it's not hard. When you ask someone else to do it for you, or you hire them to do it, you *are* personally doing it, and it's not hard. So let's turn it around and see how it feels. "It's hard for me to communicate through the Internet, e-mail, and at work"—**turn it around.** "It's not hard . . ."

PETER: It's *not* hard for me to communicate through the Internet, e-mail, and at work.

KATIE: How does that feel?

PETER: I have to get over my own pride.

KATIE: You don't *have* to. You can suffer.

PETER: I'm . . . I'm *going* to get over my own pride.

KATIE: Yes, honey, you don't have time for it! You want to do the Internet, e-mail, you want to get to work, you want to do that. Pride is costly. It's no fun, either. And you have been through a lot, so just be very gentle with yourself, take your time, and do The Work on anything that would keep you from asking another human being to help you. Do The Work on everything between you and me, whoever I am. Do The Work on every thought that would keep you from asking for help.

PETER: Okay.

KATIE: Because that's all that's stopping you. Everything you believe that would keep you from asking anyone—that's what you work on. "They'll think I'm stupid." "They'll say no." And then ask them, "Do you think I'm stupid?" Live it out and see. All it costs you is your pride. And pride is painful. So all it's going to cost you is your pain.

PETER: Right, and I'm willing to get rid of that. I look forward to it.

KATIE: Yes. Okay, then, live it out. Thank you, precious.

PETER: Thank you, Katie.

14

Seamless, unnamable,
it returns to the realm of nothing.

Ultimately, what is real can't be seen or heard or thought or grasped. You're just seeing your own eyes, hearing your own ears, reacting to the world of your own imagination. It's all created by your mind in the first place. You name it, you create it, you give it meaning upon meaning upon meaning. You add the what to reality, then you add the why. It's all you. The original is wiped out in the wave of the new, which is already old. Thought deletes anything outside itself.

Mind is so powerful that it could take the imagined fist and beat it against a wall and actually believe that you are the person whose fist it is. Because mind in its ignorance is so quick to hold its imagined world together, it has created time and space and everything in it. Mind's ability to create is a beautiful thing, unless, as the terrorist that it often is, it has created a world that's frightening or unkind. If it has, I would suggest questioning the nightmare. It doesn't matter where mind begins to question itself. " 'It's a tree'—is that true?" Or " 'I am'—is that true?" The world that mind has created can just as easily be de-created. It goes back to where it came from anyway. Your attachment to it is the only suffering.

Mind can't comprehend "nothing," the absolute, that from

which everything flows, the original non-world. To name it "noth-ing" makes it untrue. It's not "nothing," because it's prior to words. "Nothing" is not only frightening to the world of mirrored thought—it's incomprehensible. Mind becomes frightened when it considers being what it was born from, since that can never be controlled or known. Without identification as a body, mind is left to die, and death never comes for it. What never lived can never die.

Eventually, mind discovers that it's free, that it's infinitely out of control and infinitely joyful. Eventually, it falls in love with the unknown. In that it can rest. And since it no longer believes what it thinks, it remains always peaceful, wherever it is or isn't.

15

*Do you have the patience to wait
till your mud settles and the water is clear?
Can you remain unmoving
till the right action arises by itself?*

The Master can't seek fulfillment. She's already filled to the brim; there isn't room for a drop more. When you have what you want—when you *are* what you want—there's no impulse to seek anything outside yourself. Seeking is the movement away from the awareness that your life is already complete, just as it is. Even at moments of apparent pain, there's never anything wrong or lacking. Reality is always kind; what happens is the best thing that could happen. It can't be anything else, and you'll realize that very clearly if you inquire.

I have a friend whose wife fell in love with another man. He had been doing The Work for a while, and instead of going into sadness and panic, he questioned his thinking. " 'She should stay with me'—is it true? I can't know that. How do I react when I believe the thought? Extremely upset. Who would I be without the thought? I would love her and just wish the best for her." This man really wanted to know the truth. When he questioned his thinking, he found something extremely precious. "Eventually," he said, "I was able to see it as something that *should* be happening, because it was. When my wife told me about it, she didn't have to censor anything to protect me. It was amazing to hear what it was like for her, without taking any of it personally. It was the most liberating experience I ever had." His wife moved in with the other man, and he was fine with that, because he didn't want her to stay if she didn't want to. A few months later she hit a crisis point with her lover and needed someone to talk to. She went to her best friend—her husband. They calmly discussed her options. She decided to get a place of her own where she could work things out, and eventually, after many ups and downs, she went back to her husband. Through all this drama, whenever my friend found himself mentally at war with reality and experiencing pain or fear, he inquired into the thought he was believing at that moment, and returned to a calm and cheerful state of mind. He came to know for himself that the only possible problem he could have was his unquestioned thinking. His wife gave him everything he needed for his own freedom.

I often say that if I had a prayer, it would be this: *God, spare me from the desire for love, approval, or appreciation. Amen.* I don't have a prayer, of course, because I don't want anything but what I have. I know the benevolence of life. Why would I pray for something different, which would always be less than what's coming? *God* is another name for reality. It's complete, it's perfect, it fills me with the utmost joy. The thought of asking for what isn't never even arises.

But if I still believed my thoughts, I would pray for one thing first: to be spared from the desire for love. This desire causes nothing but confusion and misery. It shuts down the awareness of what you already have in reality. It's painful to seek what you can never have outside yourself. I say "can never have" because obviously you don't understand what you're seeking. If you understood it, the seeking would be over. Because you think you know what love looks like, what it should or shouldn't be, it becomes invisible to you. It's the blind seeking what doesn't exist. You beg, you plead, you bend over backward and do all sorts of other emotional acrobatics in this unending search for happy endings. Only by seeking the truth within will you find the love you can never lose. And when you find it, your natural response is appreciation.

This would be my one prayer, because the answer to it brings the end of time and space. It brings the energy of pure unlimited mind, set free in all its power and goodness. When you stop seeking love, it leaves you with nothing to do; it leaves you with the experience of being "done," in a doing that is beyond you. It's absolutely effortless. And a whole lot gets done in it, beyond what you think could ever have been accomplished.

When I don't look for approval outside me, I remain as approval. And through inquiry I have come to see that I want you to approve of what you approve of, because I love you. What you approve of is what I want. That's love—it wouldn't change anything. It already has everything it wants. It already *is* everything it wants, just the way it wants it.

16

Immersed in the wonder of the Tao,
you can deal with whatever life brings you,
and when death comes, you are ready.

You can't empty your mind of thoughts. You might as well try to empty the ocean of its water. Thoughts just keep coming back, it seems. That's the way of it.

But thoughts aren't a problem if they're met with understanding. Why would you even *want* to empty your mind, unless you're at war with reality? I love my thoughts. And if I were ever to have a stressful thought, I know how to question it and give myself peace. Even the most stressful thought could come along, and I would just be amused. You can have ten thousand thoughts a minute, and if you don't believe them, your heart remains at peace.

The original stressful thought is the thought of an I. Before that thought, there was peace. A thought is born out of nothing and instantly goes back to where it came from. If you look before, between, and after your thoughts, you'll see that there is only a vast openness. That's the space of don't-know. It's who we really are. It's the source of everything, it contains everything: life and death, beginning, middle, and end.

Until we know that death is as good as life, and that it always comes at just the right time, we're going to take on the role of God without the awareness of it, and it's always going to hurt. Whenever you mentally oppose what is, you're going to experience sadness and apparent separation. There's no sadness without a story. What is is. You *are* it.

I have a friend who, after doing inquiry sincerely for a number of years, came to understand that the world is a reflection of mind. She was married to a man who was the love of her life, and one day, while they were sitting on their couch, he had a heart attack and died in her arms. After the first shock and the tears, she began looking for grief, and there was none. For weeks she kept looking for grief, because her friends told her that grief was a necessary part of the healing process. And all she felt was a completeness: that there was nothing of him that she'd had while he was physically with her that she didn't have now.

She told me that every time a sad thought about him appeared, she would immediately ask, "Is it true?" and see the turnaround, which washed away the sadness and replaced it with what was truer. "He was my best friend; I have no one to talk to now" became "I am my best friend; I have me to talk to now." "I'll miss his wisdom" became "I don't miss his wisdom"; there was no way she could miss it, because she *was* that wisdom. Everything she thought she'd had in him she could find in herself; there was no difference. And because he turned out to be her, he couldn't die. Without the story of life and death, she said, there was just love. He was always with her.

17

The Master doesn't talk, she acts.
When her work is done,
the people say, "Amazing:
we did it, all by ourselves!"

I love being invisible. There's no responsibility in it, no one to save, no one to teach. I'm always the student: open, excited, new. I'm always filled with what's beautiful; I'm the bottomless container that always has room for more. If I had a responsibility, it would be to help you realize your own truth. You see it, you say it, it comes from within you, and I am the witness. My finger points you back to you. You're all that's left of my existence, for as long as you believe that you exist.

A friend of mine had what people call a near-death experience. She was about to enter heaven, she said, but at the last moment she was called back, and she returned to the world to save us. She didn't save herself first, *then* come back for us, which is the proper order of things. The most attractive thing about the Buddha was that he saved one person—himself. It's like the instructions on an airplane for when the pressure drops: first pull down the mask and put it over your own face, then put it over your child's.

I know what it is to enter heaven and not look back, and I know the arrogance of thinking that people need to be saved. If I can walk into the light, so can you. You can't help us with your words: "There

49

it is, over there. Follow me." No. *You* do it first, then we'll follow. This savior thing is lethal.

I don't ever see myself as a "spiritual teacher." Of course, you can use me by asking me a question. I answer you, you hear what you think I say, and you set yourself free (or not). I am your projection. I am, for you, no more and no less than your story of me. You tell the story of how I'm wonderful or how I'm terrible; you see me as an enlightened being and make me into an all-knowing guru or fairy godmother, or you see me as a Pollyannaish New Age flake, or simply as a good friend. You give me to you, or you take me from you.

All I have to offer is the four questions and turnaround. I offer them so that you can disassemble your own identity. People say, "I am so-and-so, I am solid, I am real," and though I respect that, I can never believe it. I know what I am, I know what I'm not, and I can only project that as everything. As people answer the questions, they begin to disassemble everything about who they think they are, everything frightening about their existence as they believe it to be, and in the process, as they disassemble the nightmare, they begin to notice that even the dream of what is beautiful isn't true. Until eventually there's nothing left but our own nature: brilliant, infinite, free.

People can take inquiry home with them; they can have it for breakfast every day. This deletes me as the power, and leaves me as something more powerful: an equal, an equal possibility of peace, the student sitting with the student. This is the healthiest scenario, the scenario that deletes the teacher. And aren't teachers wonderful until they're clearly seen by the mature mind?

I love it when my job is deleted! Why would I want to be seen as wise or holy? What would I have to gain by that but a story? Whatever realization I've had is for me; there's no way I can give it to you. And even if I *could* give you my realization, by that very act I would be saying, "You can't do it. I'll do it for you." I'd be teaching dependency and telling you that the answers are somewhere outside you. I have nothing for you but the questions.

18

When the great Tao is forgotten,
goodness and piety appear.

The reason I love rules and plans and religions is that people feel safe in them for a while. And, personally, I don't have any rules. I don't need them. There's a sense of order that goes on all the time as things move and change, and I am that harmony, and so are you. Not knowing is the only way to understand. That's how I discover where I'm to go next, my direction, as life lived. Why would I resist the spontaneously beautiful by trying to impose an artificial order onto it?

Meanings, rules, the whole world of right and wrong, are secondary at best. I understand how some people think they need to live by rules. Without them, they think, there's no control; if there were no rules, they think, everybody might turn out to be a murderer. And, to my eyes, rigidly pious people are doing the best they can. It's very frightening for them to watch the world unfolding in apparent chaos and not realize that the chaos itself is God in his infinite intelligence. They think that the world, the mind, needs to be encased in a structure. And I love that the structure works for them (if it does).

I used to spend a lot of time in the desert. I would just walk, with no destination. I would walk straight, even if the path turned right or left, because I understood that there was no way to be lost. I often didn't know where I was or how to get back to familiar ground. But I was living with the certainty that wherever I was, that's where I was supposed to be at that moment. This is not a theory; it's the literal truth. If I think that I'm supposed to be doing anything but what I'm doing now, I'm insane.

One day, while I was walking in the desert with some friends, we came upon a Mojave green rattlesnake, which was very rare where we were. He was coiled in front and to the right of us—big, fat, and gorgeous. And all he said was "Look: I am." I remember pointing to him and telling my friends, "Let's walk around this one." They reacted with terror, because they were stuck in a story, and they missed the beauty. The snake wisely got away from us as quickly as he could. He could have been the sand, the desert holly, the hidden waters. The earth is like a mother: quiet, unmoving, unrelenting in her honesty and kindness.

To be in the desert alone is to understand the absoluteness of solitude, the positive nature of emptiness. During the day, no sound—just mile after mile of sameness. Imagination has no context for the vastness of the desert when you're in it alone. And at night, in the moonless world, amid the smells and the silence, you lie down and have no idea what you're lying on. Is it a snake? A cactus? So you lie and wait, look up at the stars, and receive the ground, the coolness of the sand, giving up the idea that mind could grasp the lumps under your leg or your shoulder. And then the thought of time. Is it midnight? Is it five days later, five years later? And what am I who wonder what I am? And the smile that comes from knowing that you can't know and don't really care, that the answer to that would shrivel in the delight of this moment. Nothing of life imagined can compete with the beauty of nothingness, the vastness of it, the unfathomable darkness.

This amazing desert earth has been my greatest teacher. She doesn't budge from what she is. I sit on her and there is no movement, no discussion, no complaint. The earth just gives, without condition, unnoticed, and that's the proof of love. She doesn't ever with-hold. She doesn't compromise. The way she speaks is through the wind and the rain, the sand, the rocks, the sounds of her creatures. She just sings her song without meaning, and she continues to give without any expectation of return. She'll support you all your life, and if you throw a tin can onto her or dump poison into her blood-stream or drop a bomb on her, there is still total, unconditional love. She keeps giving and giving. She's me awake. She's you.

19

Throw away holiness and wisdom,
and people will be a hundred times happier.

Y ou are the wisdom you're seeking, and inquiry is a way to make that wisdom available whenever you want. My experience is that there's no one with more or with less wisdom. We all have it equally. That's the freedom I enjoy. If you think that you have a problem, you're confused.

God's will and your will are the same, whether you notice it or not. There's no mistake in the universe. It's not possible to have the concept "mistake" unless you're comparing what is with what isn't. Without the story in your mind, it's all perfect. No mistake. Strangers used to hear about me and show up at my front door (this was in 1986), and some of them would put their palms together and bow and say, "Namaste." I had never heard that before—people don't say "Namaste" in Barstow, the little desert town where I lived. So I thought they were saying, "No mistake." I was thrilled that the people coming to my door were so wise. "No mistake. No mistake.".

There's a perfect order here. "Holiness" and "wisdom" are just concepts that separate us from ourselves. We think that there's some ideal we have to strive for, as if Jesus were any holier or the Buddha any wiser than we are right now in this moment. Who would you be without your story of yourself? It's stressful to have ideals that you can achieve only in the future, a future that never comes. When you no longer believe the thought that you need to achieve anything, the world becomes a much kinder place.

Sin, too, is a concept. Think of the worst thing you ever did. Go into it as deeply as you can, from the perspective of the person you were at the time. With the limited understanding you had then, weren't you doing the best you could? How could you have done it any differently, believing what you believed? If you really enter this exercise, you'll see that nothing else is possible. The possibility that anything else could have happened is just a thought you have now about a then, an imagined past that you are comparing with the real past, which is also imagined. We're all doing the best we can. And if you feel that you've hurt someone, make amends, and thank the experience for showing you how not to live. No one would ever hurt another human being if he or she weren't confused. Confusion is the only suffering on this planet.

I was once walking through the streets of Dublin with a Catholic priest who appreciated The Work and did it on a regular basis. We came to a cathedral, he invited me in, we walked around inside the cathedral for a while, then he pointed to a little booth and said, "This is a confessional. Would you like to step in?" It seemed important to him. I said, "Yes." So he stepped into his cubicle, and I stepped into mine, and I thought, *Hmm. What do I have to confess?* I searched and searched, and nothing came. Then, through the little window, something did come: he began confessing to *me*. Later, outside the cathedral, we applied the four questions to each imagined sin and turned it around, and he said that a great weight had been lifted from him.

Everyone is doing his job. No one is more valuable than another. The things in the world that we think are so terrible are actually great teachers. There's no mistake, and there's nothing lacking. We're always going to get what we need, not what we *think* we need. Then we come to see that what we need is not only what we have, it's what we want. Then we come to want only what is. That way we always succeed, whatever happens.

20

I alone possess nothing.

You can't have an up without a down. You can't have a left without a right. This is duality. If you have a problem, you must already have the solution. The question is, Do you really want the solution, or do you want to perpetuate the problem? The solution is always there. The Work can help you find it. Write down the problem, question it, turn it around, and you have the solution.

Every thought is already over. That's grace. No thought: no problem. It's not possible to have a problem without believing a prior thought. To notice this simple truth is the beginning of peace.

I also notice that I possess nothing. Stephen slips the wedding ring onto my finger and whispers, "Try to keep it for one month." It's his little joke. He's had the experience of giving me a gift, an expensive one, that was gone the next day, because someone admired it and I knew it was theirs. He realizes that what the ring symbolizes is mine forever and that the ring itself can never belong to me, that I simply wear it until it's gone. Two years ago, I gave it to a dear, unmarried man whom we both love, but he gave it right back. So here it is, still on my left ring finger, five years later: an unexpected miracle, in Stephen's view. How can I possess anything? Things come to me only when I need them and only for as long as I need them, and the way I know I need them is that I have them.

When something's over, it's over. We all know when that point comes, and we can honor it or ignore it. When my hand reaches out for a cup of tea, I lavish myself on the whole cup of tea, though I don't know if I'm going to have one sip, three sips, ten sips, or the whole cup. When a friend gives me a gift, the gift is in the receiving. In that, it's over, and then I notice that I give the object away or keep it for a while.

I once left my purse in a restaurant in New York. I get very excited when things like that happen. I thought of the purse, my very favorite, and I thought of someone finding the cash and the wallet and the business cards and the notebook and the hand cream and the pens and the lipstick and the dental floss and the eye drops and the wonderful new cell phone and the energy bar and the pictures of my grandchildren. It's exciting to give a total stranger what you have, and to know that giving is equal to having, and that giving is also a kind of having. (This doesn't mean that I didn't cancel my credit cards.) But it was clear that the purse was supposed to belong to someone else. How did I know that she needed it? She had it. There are no accidents in my world. When you're a lover of what is, your suffering is over.

21

The Master keeps her mind
always at one with the Tao.

I have a word for God: *reality*. I call reality "God" because it rules. It is what it is, and it's so physical—it's a table, a chair, it's the shoe on your foot, it's your hair. I love God. It's so clear, so solid; it's completely dependable. You don't get a vote in what it does, and it doesn't wait for your opinion or your permission. You can trust it completely.

You can know that reality is good just as it is, because when you argue with it, you experience anxiety and frustration. Any thought that causes stress is an argument with reality. All such thoughts are variations on a theme: "Things should be different than they are." "I want . . . ," "I need . . . ," "He should . . . ," "She shouldn't . . ." It always hurts when you argue with what is.

"What is" is a story of the past. The past is past. It happened, and you can't do a thing about it. Argue with *that*! The sane alternative is to ask, "What can I do from here?" The past is a teacher, it's benign, it's over. But as long as people are living with an unquestioned past, they're living *in* the past. And it's a past that never happened in the first place. They're living in their *story* of the past. They're missing what's present right now, which is the real future. I never know what's going to happen. All I know about it is that it's a good thing.

People spend their whole lives dedicated to changing the past. It can't be done. Thinking that the past should have been different is hopeless and masochistic. "My mother should have loved me." "My child shouldn't have died." "The Holocaust shouldn't have happened." Comparing what happened to what you think should have happened is the war with God. (This is very difficult to hear when you're attached to concepts of right and wrong.) Some people even think that sadness is an act of loyalty, that it would be a betrayal of the people they love not to suffer along with them. This is crazy.

If my child has died, that's the way of it. Any argument with that brings on internal hell. "She died too soon." "I didn't get to see her grow up." "I could have done something to save her." "I was a bad mother." "God is unjust." But her death is reality. No argument in the world can make the slightest dent in what has already happened. Prayer can't change it, begging and pleading can't change it, punishing yourself can't change it, your will has no power at all. You do have the power, though, to question your thought, turn it around, and find three genuine reasons why the death of your child is equal to her not dying, or even better in the long run, both for her and for you. This takes a radically open mind, and nothing less than an open mind is creative enough to free you from the pain of arguing with what is. An open mind is the only way to peace. As long as you think that you know what should and shouldn't happen, you're trying to manipulate God. This is a recipe for unhappiness.

Reality—the way that it is, exactly as it is, in every moment—is always kind. It's our *story* about reality that blurs our vision, obscures what's true, and leads us to believe that there is injustice in the world. I sometimes say that you move totally away from reality when you believe that there is a legitimate reason to suffer. When you believe that any suffering is legitimate, you become the champion of suffering, the perpetuator of it in yourself. It's insane to believe that suffering is caused by anything outside the mind. A clear mind doesn't suffer. That's not possible. Even if you're in great physical pain, even if your beloved child dies, even if you and your family are herded off to Auschwitz, you can't suffer unless you believe an untrue thought. I'm a lover of reality. I love what is, whatever it looks like. And however it comes to me, my arms are open.

This is not to say that people shouldn't suffer. They *should* suffer, because they do. If you're feeling sad or afraid or anxious or depressed, that's what you should be feeling. To think otherwise is to argue with reality. But when you're feeling sad, for example, just notice that your sadness is the effect of believing a prior thought. Locate the thought, put it on paper and question it, for the love of truth, and then turn it around. It was you who made yourself sad—no one else—and it's you who can free yourself. This is very good news.

22

If you want to become full,
let yourself be empty.

To be empty, to surrender, to be lived by the Tao—this isn't a lofty goal that can be attained only after years of spiritual practice. When you really go inside yourself, for the love of truth, and question even one stressful concept, the mind becomes a little saner, a little more open. And you begin to see that there is no objective world out there. It's all projected. You've been living in your *story* of the world.

We want to be wonderful, generous people, but when we don't get our way, we turn into something else—in the name of goodness, of course. When we work with mind, the projector, eventually we begin to live in a state of clarity and kindness. It's possible to be kind all the time, not just when we get our way. This leaves us with a lot of energy to serve people.

As long as you believe any negative concept about one person ("He's selfish," "She's arrogant," "He shouldn't do this," "She should be that"), you're going to project it onto everyone—your husband, your wife, your parents, your children. Sooner or later, when you don't get what you want from them, or when they threaten your sacred beliefs, you're going to impose that concept onto them, until you meet it with some understanding. This is not a guess. It's what we do. We're not attached to people; we're attached to concepts about people.

61

When you truly love yourself, it's not possible to project that other people don't love you. I like to say, "When I walk into a room, I know that everyone in it loves me. I just don't expect them to realize it yet." This gets a big laugh from audiences. People are delighted at how easy it is to feel completely loved, and they see, if only for a moment, that it doesn't depend on anyone outside.

If you say that you love your husband, what does that have to do with him? You're just telling him who you are. You tell the story of how he's handsome and fascinating and sexy, and you love your story about him. You're projecting that he's your story. And then when he doesn't give you what you want, you may tell the story of how he's mean, he's controlling, he's selfish—and what does *that* have to do with him? If my husband says, "I adore you," I think, *Good. I love that he thinks I'm his sweet dream. How happy he must feel about that!* If he were ever to come to me and say, "The sorriest day of my life was when I married you," still, what would that have to do with me? He'd just be in a sad dream this time, and I might think, *Oh, poor baby, he's having a nightmare. I hope he wakes up soon.* It's not personal. How can it have anything to do with me? I love him, and if what he says about me isn't true in my experience, I'll ask him if there's anything I can do for him. If I can do it, I will, and if it's not honest for me, I won't. He is left with his story.

No one will ever understand you. Realizing this is freedom. No one will ever understand you—not once, not ever. Even at our most understanding, we can only understand our story of who you are. There's no understanding here except your own.

If you don't love another person, it hurts, because love is your very self. You can't *make* yourself do it. But when you come to love yourself, you automatically love the other person. Just as you can't make yourself love us, you can't make yourself *not* love us. It's all your projection.

When you truly love someone, a thought like "You should love me" just brings laughter to your heart. Can you hear the arrogance of that thought? "I don't care whom you want to love. You should love *me*, and I'll even trick you into it." It's the opposite of love. If I think my husband should love me, I'm insane. Whose business is it whom he loves? His, of course. The turnarounds are all I need to know: *I* should love me, and I should love *him*. Let him love whomever he loves—he's going to anyway. The story of whom someone should love keeps me from the awareness that I am what I'm seeking. It's not his job to love me—it's mine.

There's nothing you can do with love. All you can do is experience it. That's as intimate as you can ever be with another human being. You can hug him, you can kiss him, you can pack him up, take him home, cuddle him, feed him, give him your money, give him your life—and that's not it. Love is nothing you can demonstrate or prove. It's what you are. It's not a doing, it can't be "done," it's too vast to do anything with. As you open to the experience of love, it will kill who you think you are. It will have no other. It will kill anything in its way.

Once you give yourself to love, you lose your whole world as you perceived it. Love leaves nothing but itself. It's totally greedy; it has to include it all; it will not leave out even a shadow of itself. And everything else falls away, and you're like a tree losing its leaves in autumn, so beautifully. Our pain is in denying love. A boundary is an act of selfishness. There's nothing you wouldn't give to anyone if you weren't afraid. Of course, you can't be generous ahead of your time. But when you meet your thoughts with understanding, you discover that there's nothing to lose. So eventually there's no attempt at protection. Giving everything you have becomes a privilege.

The only true love affair is the one with yourself. I am married to me, and that's what I project onto everyone. I love you with all my heart; you don't even have to participate, so there's no motive in "I love you." Isn't that fine? I can love you completely, and you have nothing to do with it. There's nothing you can do to keep me from the intimacy that I experience with you.

When I say "I love you," it's self-love. There's no personality talking: I'm only talking to myself. Love is so self-absorbed that it leaves no room for any other. It's self-consuming, always. There's not a molecule separate from itself. In the apparent world of duality, people are going to see it as a you and a me, but in reality there is only one. And even that isn't true.

The voice within is what I'm married to. All marriage is a metaphor for that marriage. When I make a commitment, it's to my own truth, and there's no higher or lower. "Will you have this man to be your husband?" "I will. And I may change my mind." That's as good as it gets. I'm married only to God—reality. That's where my commitment is. It can't be to a particular person. And my husband wouldn't want it any other way.

Unless you marry the truth, there is no real marriage. Marry yourself and you have married us. We are you. That's the cosmic joke.

23

Open yourself to the Tao,
then trust your natural responses;
and everything will fall into place.

I didn't have a spiritual teacher. Of course, I've had many teachers, from my mother to my ex-husbands to my children to the stranger in rags on a corner in Santa Monica. But the privilege of not having an official teacher is that there's no tradition, so there's nothing to aspire or be loyal to. This one that I happen to be doesn't have to look like anything but what it is. It can afford to be a fool—it doesn't know anything but love. It's God delighted. It comes to take the mystery and importance out of everything. It takes the push and the time out of it.

I watch my granddaughter Marley, eleven months old, as I sing along with her musical toy—"♫ ONE TWO THREE four FIVE six SEVEN EIGHT NINE TEN ♫." She looks at me with amazed delight and then begins to dance. The dance happens beyond her control, her little diapered rear end wiggles, and she pops up and down, and her arms fly into the air. I am watching dance being invented. It's in its pristine state, it's happening for the very first time, and I can't help joining her. She, too, is my teacher. We're dancing together at the beginning of the human race, as if this were the first dance ever danced in the history of the world. She's not trying to do it right or to impress anyone. She is pure nature. And I am the same, beyond control, I begin to move in the same way, I pop up and down and my arms fly into the air. The laughter is pouring out of me. I feel so thrilled, it's the thrill of natural dance, coming from her, from me, from her. The song stops, she looks up at me, then down at the musical toy. She presses the button to begin the song again. It doesn't happen. She is figuring out how to reproduce the miracle. I watch as she presses the same button two, three times, and finally with enough force to make the music exist. At the sound of the first note she looks at me, her face lights up, her body begins to move, and the dance begins again.

My dear old white German shepherd, Kerman, was another teacher of mine, one of my greatest teachers after I got a clue in 1986. There were no conditions to her love. Toward the end of her life, her hindquarters became crippled and she couldn't walk, so when people called her, she would just drag herself along the floor to meet them. As she was dying, she began to bleed at the mouth. I called all three of my children home, and I said, "If you can't find a reason why not, I'm going to put her down." When they saw how far gone she was, they agreed that that was the best thing. So we got her favorite food, and we gave her a big party with everything she loved, and we weren't careful with her. The kids wrestled with her and called her, and she crawled to them with a puppy's smile on her face. She dragged herself across the room, apparently delighted. She didn't seem to know about pain. She didn't know about anything but giving.

When the time came to take her to the vet, we all went—nine or ten people, all her friends and family. We stood around her, and my son Ross bent down to the table, eye to eye with her. The doctor gave her the shot, a moment passed, she didn't move, and when Ross said, "She's gone," we all knew it. She had been there and then she wasn't. There was no "her" left. There was no "her" to say good-bye to. It was very sweet.

I've also learned from the trees, walking in the redwood forest, where the deer didn't run from me. I saw trees that had fallen over from wind or lightning. They appeared to be dead, and yet there was a whole world on them and in them: moss and insects and all sorts of hidden life. Even in death, they were creating and giving what was left.

Nature withholds nothing from itself, until there is nothing to give. It's like my white shepherd with the smile on her face and how when I called her she would come, dragging her hindquarters, blood dripping from her mouth. That's what we're all doing, whether or not we realize it. People have seen me crawl when the body is apparently exhausted. I never *have* to do that or anything else, ever again. I do it because it delights me. I board an airplane and feel only freedom. This awareness is my joy. It may not appear that way, but it's an internal joy that I travel with, not the apparent exhaustion. And I don't give more than anyone else. The white shepherd didn't give more, nor does the redwood. We all give equally. Without our stories, all of us are pure love.

24

He who defines himself
can't know who he really is.

Reality is very clear when your mind is clear. It couldn't be simpler, though people feel that there's got to be something hidden behind it. It's user-friendly: what you see is what you get. Whatever happens is good, and if you don't think so, you can question your mind. I see people and things without a story, so when it comes to me to move toward them or away from them, I move without argument. I don't know why not. The movement is always perfect, and I have nothing to do with it.

So, because there's nothing hidden, reality sounds like this: Woman sitting in chair with cup of tea. That's as sweet as I want it, because that's what is. I call it the last story. When you love what is, it becomes so simple to live in the world, because you understand that everything is exactly as it should be.

It's common for me to speak from the position of a personality, even though I don't believe it, from the position of mankind, from the position of earth, from the position of God, from the position of a rock. If these things even exist, I am their origin. And I'll call myself "it," because I don't have a reference point for separation. I am all those things, and I don't have any concept that I'm not. I've simply learned to speak in a way that doesn't alienate people. This leaves me as benign, unseen, unknown, as a comfortable place for people. I speak to them from the position of a friend, and if people trust me, it's because I meet them wherever they are. I'm in love. It's a love affair with itself. When mind loves itself, it loves everything it projects. To meet people where they are, without any conditions, is to meet my own self without conditions. I'm in love with everything. It's total vanity. I would kiss the ground I walk on—it's all me.

I like speaking as a human. I call it my disguise. The first thing I did when I woke up to reality was to fall in love with form. I fell in love with the eyes and the floor and the ceiling. I am that. I am that. It's nothing, and it's everything. None of it is separate. Just to be born into this goodness, right now, with eyes open, is enough.

As I gaze out at the sky on this perfect day, I don't even know it's a sky until mind names it. In that moment, it comes into existence. There is no world to see until mind "I"s me and begins to produce names that, to an unquestioned mind, would separate reality into this, this, this, this. I love that my mind doesn't believe my mind. Without meaning, how can separation exist? I appear as the old and the new, the beginning and the end, I'm you, I'm everything—this ecstatic pulse, this nameless joy, this dancing without movement, this electrifying brilliant nothingness.

25

There was something formless and perfect
before the universe was born.

In the beginning was the word. It happens when you wake up in the morning. The word is yours. That's how the world is created.

Before the beginning, there is only reality, formless and perfect, solitary, infinite, free. There's no name for it, there's no ripple of a name. The name *is* the ripple. In the ripple the whole lake arises. No ripple, no lake.

What's real is nameless. It doesn't change, it doesn't flow, it doesn't leave or return, it doesn't even exist, it's beyond existence or non-existence. If you call it something, you get nothing. So call it "the Tao" if you like; that's as good a name as any. Whatever you call it, that isn't it. And it's always a beginning.

26

The Master travels all day
without leaving home.
However splendid the views,
she stays serenely in herself.

Peace is our natural condition. Only by believing an untrue thought is it possible to move from peace into emotions like sadness and anger. Without the pull of beliefs, the mind stays serenely in itself and is available for whatever comes along.

Who would you be in people's presence without, for example, the story that anyone should care about you, ever? You would be love itself. When you believe the myth that people should care, you're too needy to care about people or about yourself. The experience of love can't come from anyone else; it can come only from inside you.

I was once walking in the desert with a man who began to have a stroke. We sat down, and he said, "Oh my God, I'm dying. *Do* something!" He was talking through one side of his mouth because the other side had become paralyzed. What I did was just sit there beside him, loving him, looking into his eyes, knowing that we were miles from a phone or car. He said, "You don't even care, do you?" I said, "No." And through his tears, he started to laugh, and I did, too. And eventually his faculties returned; the stroke had come to pass, not to stay. This is the power of love. I wouldn't leave him for a caring.

If someone were knifed in front of me, what would compassion look like? I would do everything within my power to help, of course, but to think that this shouldn't be happening would be to argue with reality. That's not efficient. If I cared, I couldn't be the intimacy that I am. A caring would move me away from the real, would separate me from the one who is stabbed and from the one with the knife, and I am everything. To exclude anything that appears in your universe is not love. Love joins with everything. It doesn't exclude the monster. It doesn't avoid the nightmare—it looks forward to it, because, like it or not, it may happen, if only in your mind. There's no way that I would let caring interfere with what I experience as my very own self. It has to include every cell, every atom. It *is* every cell and every atom. There is no "also."

When something feels right, I do it; I live my life out of *that* caring. That's how I contribute to life: by picking up the trash on the sidewalk, by recycling, sitting with the homeless, sitting with the wealthy, helping people who are deeply confused question their thinking. I love what is and how it changes through my hands and yours. It's wonderful to be so available to change what I can, and for it to be effortless, always.

Some people think that compassion means feeling another person's pain. That's nonsense. It's not possible to feel another person's pain. You imagine what you'd feel if you were in that person's shoes, and you feel your own projection. Who would you be without your story? Pain-free, happy, and totally available if someone needs you—a listener, a teacher in the house, a Buddha in the house, the one who lives it. As long as you think there's a you and a me, let's get the bodies straight. What I love about separate bodies is that when you hurt, I don't—it's not my turn. And when I hurt, you don't. Can you be there for me without putting your own suffering between us? Your suffering can't show me the way. Suffering can only teach suffering.

The Buddhists say that it's important to recognize the suffering in the world, and that's true, of course. But if you look more deeply, even that is a story. It's a story to say that there is any suffering in the world. Suffering is imagined, because we haven't adequately questioned our thoughts. I am able to be present with people in extreme states of torment without seeing their suffering as real. I'm in the position of being totally available to help them see what I see, if that's what they want. They're the only ones who can change, but I can be present, with kind words and the power of inquiry.

It's amazing how many people believe that suffering is a proof of love. *If I don't suffer when you suffer,* they think, *it means that I don't love you.* How can that possibly be true? Love is serene; it's fearless. If you're busy projecting what someone's pain must feel like, how can you be fully present with her? How can you hold her hand and love her with all your heart as she moves through her experience of pain? Why would she want you to be in pain, too? Wouldn't she rather have you present and available? You can't be present for people if you believe that you're feeling their pain. If a car runs over someone and you project what that must feel like, you're paralyzed. But sometimes in a crisis like that, the mind loses its reference, it can't project anymore, you don't think, you just act, you run over and pick up the car before you have time to think *This isn't possible.* It happens in a split second. Who would you be without your story? The car is up in the air.

Sadness is always a sign that you're believing a stressful thought that isn't true for you. It's a constriction, and it feels bad. Conventional wisdom says differently, but the truth is that sadness isn't rational, it isn't a natural response, and it can't ever help you. It just indicates the loss of reality, the loss of the awareness of love. Sadness is the war with what is. It's a tantrum. You can experience it only when you're arguing with God. When the mind is clear, there isn't any sadness. There can't be.

If you move into situations of loss in a spirit of surrender to what is, all you experience is a profound sweetness and an excitement about what can come out of the apparent loss. And once you question the mind, once the stressful story is seen for what it is, there's nothing you can do to make it hurt. You see that the worst loss you've experienced is the greatest gift you can have. When the story arises again—"She shouldn't have died" or "He shouldn't have left"—it's experienced with a little humor, a little joy. Life is joy, and if you understand the illusion arising, you understand that it's you arising, as joy.

What does compassion look like? At a funeral, just eat the cake. You don't have to know what to do. It's revealed to you. Someone comes into your arms, and the kind words speak themselves; you're not doing it. Compassion isn't a doing. Whether or not you're suffering over their suffering, you're standing or you're sitting. But one way you're comfortable, the other way you're not.

You don't have to feel bad to act kindly. On the contrary: the less you suffer, the kinder you naturally become. And if compassion means wanting others to be free of suffering, how can you want for others what you won't give to yourself?

I read an interview with a well-known Buddhist teacher in which he described how appalled and devastated he felt while watching the planes hit the World Trade Center on September 11, 2001. While this reaction is very popular, it is not the reaction of an open mind and heart. It has nothing to do with compassion. It comes from believing unquestioned thoughts. He believed, for example, "This shouldn't be happening" or "This is a terrible thing." It was thoughts like these that were making him suffer, not the event itself. He was devastating *himself* with his unquestioned thoughts. His suffering had nothing to do with the terrorists or the people who died. Can you take this in? Here was a man dedicated to the Buddha's way—the end of suffering—who in that moment was terrorizing his own mind, causing his own grief. I felt compassion for people who projected fearful meanings onto that picture of a plane hitting a building, who killed themselves with their unquestioned thoughts and took away their own state of grace.

The end of suffering happens in this very moment, whether you're watching a terrorist attack or doing the dishes. And compassion begins at home. Because I don't believe my thoughts, sadness can't exist.

That's how I can go to the depths of anyone's suffering, if they invite me, and take them by the hand and walk them out of it into the sunlight of reality. I've taken the walk myself.

I've heard people say that they cling to their painful thoughts because they're afraid that without them they wouldn't be activists for peace. "If I felt completely peaceful," they say, "why would I bother taking action at all?" My answer is "Because that's what love does." To think that we need sadness or outrage to motivate us to do what's right is insane. As if the clearer and happier you get, the less kind you become. As if when someone finds freedom, she just sits around all day with drool running down her chin. My experience is the opposite. Love is action. It's clear, it's kind, it's effortless, and it's irresistible.

27

What is a good man but a bad man's teacher?
What is a bad man but a good man's job?
If you don't understand this, you will get lost,
however intelligent you are.
It is the great secret.

How can I not be available to anyone who asks me for help? I love people just the way they are, whether they see themselves as saints or sinners. I know that each of us is beyond categories, unfathomable. It's not possible to reject people unless you believe your story about them. And, really, I don't accept or reject; I welcome everyone with open arms.

This doesn't mean that I condone the harm that people do, or any form of unkindness. But no one is bad by nature. When someone harms another human being, it's because he or she is confused. This is as true of ordinary people as of the murderers and rapists I work with in prisons. They've been protecting—to the death—the sacred, stressful thoughts that they believe.

If I see a mother hitting her child, for example, I don't stand by and let it happen, and I don't lecture the mother. She is innocently acting from a belief system she hasn't questioned. Because she believes her stressful thoughts—"The child is disrespectful," "He isn't listening," "He shouldn't talk back," "He shouldn't have done what he did," "He needs to be forced into submission"—she has to strike out. It's very painful to be confused. So when I see the mother, who is me, hitting the child, who is me, my way is to move to the mother, because she's the cause of the problem. I might go up to her and say, "Can I help?" or maybe "I know how painful it is to hit your own child. I have done that, too. I've been there. Would you like to talk about it?" Love doesn't stand by—it moves with the speed of clarity. It includes both the mother and the child. To help the mother work with her thoughts is also to help the child. And I know that ultimately I'm not doing it for either of them, I'm doing it for myself, for my own sense of what's right. So activism becomes very personal, and in my experience it's more effective with a clear mind and no agenda.

It's the same with any commitment. I keep my commitments to people because they're commitments to me. They're *my* business: they have nothing to do with the other person. Several years ago, when I was in Cologne, a German friend of mine asked me to come to the hospice as quickly as possible. He was dying, and he said that his dearest wish was for me to hold his hand and look into his eyes as he died. "Of course," I said. "I'll come right away." The hospice was in another city, about an hour's drive away. Another German friend offered to be my driver. His hidden agenda was to do some errands in the city while I sat with the dying man.

When we got close to the hospice, he began to ask pedestrians for directions to where he wanted to go. I reminded him that I had a commitment to keep. He disregarded me and kept asking for directions. I tapped him on the shoulder, looked straight into his eyes, and very clearly told him, "Please start the car. I need to go to the hospice now." He paid no attention. After five minutes or so, when he had gotten the directions, he drove on and dropped me off at the hospice. I hurried to the door and knocked. Two very grave nuns appeared. I introduced myself, and they said that I was too late: Gerhard had just died.

I had the thought, "Ah, I'm too late," and simultaneously a wordless *Is it true?* rose up to meet it. I felt a warm inner smile. If I had believed that I was too late, I might have felt sad, disappointed, angry at my driver, angry at myself for trusting him to get me there right away, and even devastated that I had let Gerhard down at the moment of his death. But I am always sure that reality's timing is better than mine. I had done my best, and this was obviously the perfect moment for me to arrive, neither too early nor too late.

I told the nuns that I wanted to go to Gerhard's room, and they led me there. I sat down beside him. His eyes were wide open; he looked surprised. I held his hand, sat with him, and had a silent, wonderful visit. I love keeping my commitments.

28

Know the male,
yet keep to the female:
receive the world in your arms.

Without a story, I'm neither personal nor impersonal, neither male nor female. There's no word for what I am. To call it nothing is as untrue as to call it something. Who needs a name for it, in the middle of life and death? It does what it does: it eats, sleeps, cooks, cleans, talks to a friend, and goes its own way, delighted.

I love what I think, and I'm never tempted to believe it. Thoughts are like the wind or the leaves on the trees or the raindrops falling. They're not personal, they don't belong to us, they just come and go. When they're met with understanding, they're friends. I love my stories. I love being a woman, even though I'm not. I love the way my sixty-three-year-old body flows and opens. I love the feminine symbols, the beautiful clothes and textures, the earrings, how they flash and dangle, the necklaces, the colors, the fragrance of the perfumes, the feel of the shampoos and soaps. I love the softness and smoothness of my skin. (Sometimes I'll be stroking Stephen's hand for ten minutes before I discover that it's my hand.) I love how generous the skin is, how efficiently my organs work, the elegance of my legs. Sometimes, as I raise my arm reaching for a sweater, I happen to see my breasts, and the delight that I experience is immense. *How is it possible to project such a gorgeous body?* I think. *How beautiful and strange!*

When Stephen touches me, it's shock and surprise, over and over. I don't interrupt it by thinking about its end, I give myself no internal explanation of what is happening, what the touch means—I just feel its power and warmth, the inner strength with each wave of feeling. It's the experience of opening to the beloved; it's everything; it's the unknown, the uncensored, the unending, the not-to-be-survived, opening fearlessly to the next wave and the next. Each response that appears in reaction to the touch, in touching the other, is a mystery. And just when I think that it can't open any more, it opens again. I don't know what it is or what I'm touching or what is touching me; I only know that it's always new and good beyond explanation, and I love the textures, shapes, softnesses, smells, flavors, the natural fit and flow of each part, the other's reaction to it, his strength to receive; it's all one intensity, and body becomes like a wire filled with electricity, a live electrical cord without conduit to hold it in place, and I never know or care where the body—my body, his—will go or what is happening or what will happen; awareness is always alive, awake in the stillness, unaffected, ever-present, noticing, focusing, watching, *as* that timeless change, as its own miracle.

29

The world is sacred.
It can't be improved.
If you tamper with it, you'll ruin it.
If you treat it like an object, you'll lose it.

The world is perfect. As you question your mind, this becomes more and more obvious. Mind changes, and as a result, the world changes. A clear mind heals everything that needs to be healed. It can never be fooled into believing that there is one speck out of order.

But some people take the insight that the world is perfect and make it into a concept, and then they conclude that there's no need to get involved in politics or social action. That's separation. If someone came to you and said, "I'm suffering. Please help me," would you answer, "You're perfect just the way you are," and turn away? Our heart naturally responds to people and animals in need.

Realization has no value until it's lived. I would travel to the ends of the earth for the sake of one person who is suffering. The desperate, the hopeless, are unenlightened cells of my own body. It's my own body I'm talking about—the body of the world is *my* body. Would I let myself drown in water that doesn't exist? Would I let myself die in an imagined torture chamber? *My God,* I think, *there's someone out there who really believes there's a problem.* I remember when I used to think there was a problem. How can I say no when that person asks for help? That would be saying no to myself. So I say yes and I go, if I can. It's a privilege. It's more than that: it's self-love.

People *are* perfect just the way they are, however deeply they're suffering, but they don't realize that yet. So when I meet someone who's suffering, I don't say, "Oh, there's no problem, everything is perfect." Though I can see that there's never a problem, and I'm available to help him see that, telling him what I see would be unkind. That part of my body is suffering, everything is *not* perfect for him, because he believes it's not. I, too, have been trapped in the torture chamber of the mind. I hear what he thinks he needs, I hear his sadness or despair, and I'm available. That's full-blown activism. In the presence of someone who doesn't see a problem, the problem falls away—which shows you that there isn't a problem.

People ask me, "How can you listen to all these problems, day after day, year after year? Doesn't it drain your energy?" Well, it doesn't. I've questioned my stressful thoughts, and I've seen that every single one of them is untrue. Every thought that used to look like a poisonous snake is actually a rope. I could stand over that rope for a thousand years, and never be frightened of it again. I see clearly what some people don't yet see for themselves. Everyone in the world might come upon that rope and run screaming the other way, and I wouldn't be afraid for them, feel sorry for them, or worry about them at all, because I realize that they're not in danger, they're absolutely not in harm's way. As they cry snake, I see only rope.

If you have a problem with people or with the state of the world, I invite you to put your stressful thoughts on paper and question them, and to do it for the love of truth, not in order to save the world. Turn it around: save your own world. Isn't that why you want to save the world in the first place? So that you can be happy? Well, skip the middleman, and be happy from here! You're it. You're the one. In this turnaround you remain active, but there's no fear in it, no internal war. So it ceases to be war trying to teach peace. War can't teach peace. Only peace can.

I don't try to change the world—not ever. The world changes by itself, and I'm a part of that change. I'm absolutely, totally, a lover of what is. When people ask me for help, I say yes. We inquire, and they begin to end their suffering, and in that they begin to end the suffering of the world.

I stand in my own truth and don't presume to know what's best for the planet. Knowing that the world is perfect doesn't mean that you withdraw or stop doing what you know is right for you to do. If, for example, you're concerned about the environment, please give us all the facts. Do a whole study of it, go to graduate school if you have to, help us out here. And if you talk to us clearly, without an agenda or any investment in the results, we can hear you, because you're on our level. You're not talking to us from a superior, I-know position. If you know that we're all equal, that we're all doing the best we can, you can be the most powerful activist on the planet.

Love is the power. I know only one way to be an activist who can really penetrate the human race, and that is to give the facts, to tell your experience honestly, and to love without condition. You can't convince the world of anything, even if it's for the world's own good, because eventually your righteousness will be seen through, and then you're on a stage debating a corporate polluter, and you start pointing your finger in outrage. That's what you've been hiding when you believe "I know what's best for the planet."

When you attack a corporate official for destroying the atmosphere, however valid your information, do you think that he'll be open to what you're saying? You're threatening him with your attitude, and the facts can get lost, because you're coming from fear and righteous anger. All he'll hear is that you think he's doing it wrong, it's his fault, and he'll go into denial and resistance. But if you speak to him without stress, in total confidence that everything is just the way it should be in this very moment, you'll be able to express yourself kindly, effectively, and with no fear about the future.

Violence teaches only violence. Stress teaches stress. If you clean up your mental environment, we'll clean up our physical one much more quickly. That's how it works. And if you do that genuinely, without violence in your heart, without anger, without pointing at corporations as the enemy, then people begin to notice. We begin to listen and notice that change through peace is possible. It has to begin with one person. If you're not the one, who is?

The world will test you in every way, so that you can realize that last little piece that's unfinished inside you. It's a perfect setup. Checkmate.

30

*She understands that the universe
is forever out of control,
and that trying to dominate events
goes against the current of the Tao.*

How do we respond to a world that seems out of control? The world seems that way because it *is* out of control—the sun rises whether we want it to or not, the toaster breaks, someone cuts you off on your way to work. We've never had control. We have the *illusion* of control when things go the way we think they should. And when they don't, we say we've lost control, and we long for some sort of enlightened state beyond all this, where we imagine we'll have control again. But what we really want is peace. We think that by having control or becoming "enlightened" (and no one knows what that means) we'll find peace.

Before I woke up to reality in 1986, I had a symbol for that: my children's socks. Every morning they would be on the floor, and every morning I would have the thought, "My children should pick up their socks." It was my religion. You could say that my world was accelerating out of control—in my mind there were socks everywhere. And I would be filled with rage and depression because I believed that these socks didn't belong on the floor (even though, morning after morning, that's where they were) and that it was my children's job to pick them up (even though, morning after morning, they didn't). I use the symbol of socks, but you might find that for you the same thoughts apply to the environment or politics or money. We think that these things should be different than they are right now, and we suffer because we believe our thoughts.

At forty-three, after ten years of deep depression and despair, my real life began. What I came to see was that my suffering wasn't a result of not having control; it was a result of arguing with reality. I discovered that when I believed my thoughts, I suffered, but that when I didn't believe them, I didn't suffer, and that this is true for every human being. Freedom is as simple as that. I found that suffering is optional. I found a joy within me that has never disappeared, not for a single moment. That joy is in everyone, always. When you question your mind for the love of truth, your life always becomes happier and kinder.

Inquiry helps the suffering mind move out of its arguments with reality. It helps us move into alignment with constant change. After all, the change is happening anyway, whether we like it or not. Everything changes, it seems. But when we're attached to our thoughts about how that change should look, being out of control feels uncomfortable.

Through inquiry, we enter the area where we do have control: our thinking. We question our thoughts about the ways in which the world seems to have gone crazy, for example. And we come to see that the craziness was never in the world, but in us. The world is a projection of our own thinking. When we understand our thinking, we understand the world, and we come to love it. In that, there's peace. Who would I be without the thought that the world needs improving? Happy where I am right now: the woman sitting on a chair in the sunlight. Pretty simple.

My children pick up their socks now, they tell me. They understand now, they love me without condition, because when I became quiet they could hear themselves. Everything I undo, they have to undo; they are me, living out what I believed. The apparent world is like an echo. The echo went out from me for forty-three years, and now it's coming back. It's all like a breath, like a lake when you toss a pebble in, the ripples going out all those years and now they're coming back. I undid the turmoil, and my children are losing it also. They're losing their attachment to so many of the concepts I taught them; they're becoming quiet. And that's what The Work does for everyone. That's what I mean by coming back into itself.

The apparent craziness of the world, like everything else, is a gift that we can use to set our minds free. Any stressful thought that you have about the planet, for example, shows you where you are stuck, where your energy is being exhausted in not fully meeting life as it is, without conditions. You can't free yourself by finding a so-called enlightened state outside your own mind. When you question what you believe, you eventually come to see that you are the enlightenment you've been seeking. Until you can love what is—everything, including the apparent violence and craziness—you're separate from the world, and you'll see it as dangerous and frightening. I invite everyone to put these fearful thoughts on paper, question them, and set themselves free. When mind is not at war with itself, there's no separation in it. I'm sixty-three years old and unlimited. If I had a name, it would be Service. If I had a name, it would be Gratitude.

You may find that you don't need to navigate a future at all—that what appears now is all you've got, and even this is always immediately gone. And when you've stopped making war with reality, you *are* what changes, totally without control. That state of constant change is creation without limits—efficient, free, and beautiful beyond description.

31

Weapons are the tools of fear.

Defense is the first act of war. When people used to say, "Katie, you don't listen," I would immediately bristle and respond, "Of course I listen! How dare you say that! Who do you think you are? I listen!" I didn't realize that *I* was the one making war by defending myself. And I was the one who could end it. It doesn't take two people to end war; it takes only one.

The personality hates criticism and loves agreement. Actually, for the personality, love *is* nothing more than agreement. A relationship is two people who agree with each other's stories. If I agree with you, you love me. And the minute I don't agree with you, the moment I question one of your sacred beliefs, I become your enemy; you divorce me in your mind. Then you start looking for all the reasons why you're right, and you stay focused outside yourself. When you're focused outside and believe that your problem is caused by someone else, rather than by your attachment to the story you're believing in the moment, you are your own victim, and the situation appears to be hopeless.

Your partner is your mirror. Except for the way you perceive him, he doesn't even exist for you. He is who you see he is, and ultimately it's just you again, thinking. It's just you, over and over and over, and in this way you remain blind to yourself and feel justified and lost. To think that your partner is anything but a mirror of you is painful. So, when you see him as flawed in any way, you can be sure that that's where your own flaw is. The flaw has to be in your thinking, because you're the one projecting it. You are always what you judge us to be in the moment. There's no exception. You are your own suffering; you are your own happiness.

There's no way to truly join your partner except by getting free of your belief that you need something from him that he's not giving. Nothing can cost you someone you love. There's nothing your husband can possibly do to keep you from loving him. The only way you can lose him is by believing what you think. You're one with your husband until you believe that he should look a certain way, he should give you something, he should be something other than what he is. That's how you divorce him. Right then and there, you have lost your marriage.

Of course, sometimes it's best to physically leave. If your husband is abusive, question your thoughts about why you stay. As you enlighten yourself to what's true, you may come to see that the only sane choice is to leave him. You may love him with all your heart and simply know not to live with him. We don't have to be fearful, bitter, or angry to end a marriage. Or, if you're not ready to leave, you may stay in the marriage, but with a greater awareness of how you're abusing yourself by allowing him to abuse you. It's like a yard with a big sign on the gate: THIS DOG BITES. If you walk into the yard once and are bitten, the dog has bitten you. If you walk into the yard a second time and are bitten, you have bitten you. This very awareness can change everything. By questioning your mind, you begin to realize that ultimately no one can hurt you—only you can. You see that you are 100 percent responsible for your own happiness. This is very good news.

If my husband were to have an affair and that were not okay with me, I would say, "Sweetheart, I understand that you're having an affair, and I notice that when you do that, something inside me tends to move away from you. I don't know what that is, I only know that it's so; it mirrors your movement away from me, and I want you to know that." And then if he were to continue his affair, to prefer to spend his time with another woman, I might notice that I was moving away, but I wouldn't have to leave him in anger. There is nothing I can do to stay with him, and there is nothing I can do to divorce him. I'm not running this show. I might stay with him, or I might divorce him in a state of total love, and think, *This is fascinating; we promised we would be together always, and I'm divorcing him now,* and I would probably laugh, love that he has what he wants, and move on, because there is no war in me. And someone else would divorce her husband thinking, "He shouldn't have had the affair," "He hurt me," "He doesn't deserve me," "He broke his promises," "He's heartless." Either way, the movement is the same; the only difference is the story. You're going to make the trip either way. The question is, Are you going to go kicking and screaming, or are you going to go with dignity, generosity, and peace? You can't dictate this, you can't fake it, you can't make yourself be spiritual or loving. Just be honest and question your thinking. Then, eventually, when people say, "Oh, it's a terrible thing, this divorce," you might respond, "I understand how you see it that way, and that's not my experience at all."

It doesn't take two people to end war in a marriage; it takes only one. And if two people have ended it, life can be twice as beautiful.

I come in after work and open the refrigerator door. My favorite snack is waiting for me. I know the exact place where I put it: on the top shelf, to the right . . . It's not there! He ate it! I feel an inner chuckle. There are no stressful thoughts, such as "He's inconsiderate, he knew it was mine, I was so looking forward to eating it, and he ruined it all." Not a snack attack: a thought attack! If I had these thoughts and believed them, I'd begin to feel annoyed at Stephen, maybe even angry and resentful. The reality is that I instantly understand it's better for me that he did eat my snack. In fact, I'm glad he ate it. I can't help smiling. Even though I wasn't aware of it at the time, it turns out that I bought it for *him*. I'm delighted to know that I was so considerate. And I'm also considerate to myself in seeing things this way.

When Stephen comes home, I tell him. We both laugh. He says he didn't realize I had bought the snack for myself. I tell him how glad I am that he ate it, and I also ask him to check with me next time, to see if in fact it's for him. He agrees. I realize that he might remember this and he might not. I'm thrilled to see that what I planned fell short of reality. I had imagined eating the snack myself, and something even sweeter happened.

32

If powerful men and women
could remain centered in the Tao,
all things would be in harmony.

As you lose the filter that I call a story, you begin to see reality as it is: simple, brilliant, and kinder than you could have imagined. There's a resonance that doesn't ever leave the center. You come to honor it, because you realize that you have no authentic life outside it.

Wherever you stand, you're in the center of the universe. There's neither big nor small. Galaxies and electrons exist only in your own perception. Everything revolves around you. Everything goes out from you and returns to you.

This may seem like selfishness. But it's the opposite of selfishness: it's total generosity. It's love for everyone and everything you meet, because you've been enlightened to yourself. There's nothing kinder than knowing you're It. The awareness of your own self—the only self that has ever existed or ever will exist—leaves you automatically centered. You become your own love affair. You're self-amazed, self-delighted. You're all alone, forever. Don't you love it? *Look* at your beautiful self!

I used to believe that there was a you and a me. Then I discovered that there's no you, that in fact you are me. There aren't two to take care of, or three, or four, or a billion. There's only one. The relief of that! It's enormous! "You mean there's nothing to do? That if I'm okay, everything is okay?" Yes, that's exactly it. It's self-realization. Everything falls sweetly, effortlessly, into your lap.

You're not only the center, you're the circumference. You're the whole circle, and you're everything outside the circumference, too. Nothing can limit or circumscribe you. You're all of it. You're all that you can possibly imagine—inside, outside, up, down. Nothing exists that doesn't come out of you. Do you understand? If it doesn't come out of you, it cannot exist. What are you manifesting? Stars? Universes? A tree? A bird? A stone? Well, who is the thinker? Take a look: Did anything exist before you thought it? When you're asleep and not dreaming, where is the world?

When I first realized there was only me, I began to laugh, and the laughter ran deep. I preferred reality to denial. And that was the end of sorrow.

33

If you stay in the center
and embrace death with your whole heart,
you will endure forever.

A doctor once took a sample of my blood and came back to me with a long face. He said he was bringing bad news; he was very sorry, but I had cancer. Bad news? I couldn't help laughing. When I looked at him, I saw that he was quite taken aback. Not everyone understands this kind of laughter. Later, it turned out that I didn't have cancer, and that was good news too.

The truth is that until we love cancer, we can't love God. It doesn't matter what symbols we use—poverty, loneliness, loss—it's the concepts of good and bad that we attach to them that make us suffer. I was sitting once with a friend who had a huge tumor, and the doctors had given her just a few weeks to live. As I was leaving her bedside, she said, "I love you," and I said, "No, you don't. You can't love me until you love your tumor. Every concept that you put onto that tumor, you'll eventually put onto me. The first time I don't give you what you want, or threaten what you believe, you'll put that concept onto me." This might sound harsh, but my friend had asked me to always tell her the truth. The tears in her eyes were tears of gratitude, she said.

No one knows what's good and what's bad. No one knows what death is. Maybe it's not a something; maybe it's not even a nothing. It's the pure unknown, and I love that. We imagine that death is a state of being or a state of nothingness, and we frighten ourselves with our own concepts. I'm a lover of what is: I love sickness and health, coming and going, life and death. I see life and death as equal. Reality is good; so death must be good, whatever it is, if it's anything at all.

A few months ago I was visiting Needles, the small desert town in southern California where my daughter, Roxann, lives. I was at the grocery store with her when some old friends of the family whom I hadn't seen for decades spotted me. "Katie!" they called out, and they came up to me, beaming. They hugged me, they asked how I was, I told them, and then they asked, "And how is your dear mother doing?" I said, "She's wonderful. She's dead." Silence. Suddenly the smiles were gone. I saw that they were having a problem, but I didn't know what it was. When Roxann and I were outside the store, she turned to me and said, "Mom, when you talk to people like that, they can't handle it." That hadn't occurred to me. I was just telling the truth.

Until you experience death as a gift, your work's not done. So if you're afraid of it, that shows you what to question next. There's nothing else to do; you're either believing these childish stories, or you're questioning them—there's no other choice. What's not okay about dying? You close your eyes every night, and you go to sleep. People look forward to it; some people actually prefer that part. And that's as bad as it gets, except for your belief that says there's some-thing else. Before a thought, there's no one, nothing—only peace that doesn't even recognize itself as peace.

What I know about dying is that when there's no escape, when you know that no one is coming to save you, there's no fear. You just don't bother. The worst thing that can happen on your deathbed is a belief. Nothing worse than that has ever happened. So if you are lying on your deathbed and the doctor says it's all over for you and you believe him, all the confusion stops. You no longer have anything to lose. And in that peace, there is only you.

People who know there's no hope are free; decisions are out of their hands. It has always been that way, but some people have to die bodily to find out. No wonder they smile on their deathbeds. Dying is everything they were looking for in life: they've given up the delusion of being in charge. When there's no choice, there's no fear. They begin to realize that nothing was ever born but a dream and nothing ever dies but a dream.

When you're clear about death, you can be totally present with someone who's dying, and no matter what kind of pain she appears to be experiencing, it doesn't affect your happiness. You're free to just love her, to hold her and care for her, because it's your nature to do that. To come to that person in fear is to teach fear: she looks into your eyes and gets the message that she is in deep trouble. But if you come in peace, fearlessly, she looks into your eyes and sees that whatever is happening is good.

Dying is just like living. It has its own way, and you can't control it. People think, *I want to be conscious when I die.* That's hopeless. Even wanting to be conscious ten minutes from now is hopeless. You can only be conscious now. Everything you want is here in this moment.

I like to tell a story about a friend of mine who was waiting for a revelation just before he died, saving his energy, trying to be completely conscious. Finally his eyes widened, he gasped, and he said, "Katie, we are larvae." Profound awareness on his deathbed. I said, "Sweetheart, is that true?" And the laughter simply poured out of him. The revelation was that there *was* no revelation. Things are fine just as they are; only a concept can take that away from us. A few days later he died, with a smile on his face.

I had another friend who was dying and felt sure he knew when his last moment was coming. But we die at exactly the right time—not an instant too soon or too late. This man was intent on doing the

Tibetan Book of the Dead thing, and his friends had promised to come to his bedside and do the rituals from the book. When he called them, they all came, and they went through the rituals, and then he didn't die. They went home, and a few days later, once again, he was sure he knew when his last moment was coming; the friends showed up, they did all the rituals again, and again he didn't die. The same thing happened two or three more times, and finally everyone was thinking, *When is this guy going to do it?* They had been called so many times! It was like the boy who cried wolf. He asked me if I would be there on such-and-such a day for so many hours, and I said, "If I can get there, I will." But as he was dying, finally, the people he left in charge didn't even bother to call me. It wasn't the way he'd planned; it was perfect instead.

Oh, stories—I love them! What else *is* there?

34

The great Tao flows everywhere.

Mind appears to flow everywhere, but it is the unmoving, the never-having-moved. It appears as everything. Eventually it sees that nowhere is where it is.

Its unceasing work is self-realization. It feels humble, because it sees that what hasn't been created can't be claimed. The splendor of humility is all that it's left with. It's left in a state of gratitude for everything: for itself.

As mind realizes one world after another, it realizes non-existence, and thus it can't hold on to anything. There's nothing to hold on to, and that is its freedom. It constantly begins again, in the unlimited un-worlds of the self—ordinary, balanced, centered, the beginning, the end.

35

She who is centered in the Tao
can go where she wishes, without danger.
She perceives the universal harmony,
even amid great pain,
because she has found peace in her heart.

You don't have to think in order to be okay. We're not doing the thinking; we're being thought. There's nothing to know, so you don't have to pretend that you know anything. You're absolutely safe. There's nothing you can do to live, and nothing you can do to die.

If you're centered in reality, you can go where you wish without danger. It's not an act of courage. There's no risk involved, because danger happens only in the future, and the future can never come. Nothing is ultimately real, so when people talk about violence, I notice the violence that they're using, right now, against reality. Why would you be afraid of reality? Reality is benign for those who can see clearly.

Once, not long after I woke up in 1986, a Christian minister said to me, "You're too open. You don't have any boundaries or resistance, and that's dangerous. Evil entities could walk in and take you over, because all your doors are open, and they could do you and the rest of us terrible harm." I was like a baby in those days: I almost always believed people. But when this man spoke about evil, I knew that what he was saying wasn't possible. I believed him when he said there were such things as entities, because at that point I had no reason not to. But to me, "evil" meant "confused." Anyone who thinks that evil exists is frightened and therefore confused. And I knew that everything is welcome here—everything. This body isn't mine, and anything that needs to enter is welcome. I delight in that. What could possibly enter that could survive the truth? Truth is the power that sets us free, and there is nothing anyone can do about that. There *is* nothing terrible in the world. Evil is just one more story to keep us from opening to love. What I know is that God is everything and God is good.

I can go anywhere, because everything is a metaphor to me; it's all internal. The external is my internal. There's no way I couldn't live a fearless life. I'm rooted in reality. I love it, and I can't project anything but love.

Jerusalem: I get an invitation to Gaza from a Palestinian man who has just attended one of my events. Yes, of course I'll go, I don't know why not. My Orthodox Jewish Israeli friends say, "No, no, you can't, it's very dangerous, the poverty is appalling, they're desperate, violent people, they won't like it that you teach Jews, you might not be allowed back into Israel." They are very attached to their stories, and they think they're trying to rescue me. They don't realize that their stories are all about a non-existent future. None of them is valid for me. I listen with an open mind, and because I can't believe what they believe, I continue to make arrangements to meet my new Arab friend on the other side of the wall.

And, oh, what a wall and a checkpoint it is! I enter Gaza, and the sewers are running open in the streets, there are twenty or thirty people living in a two-room apartment, some of the buildings have huge, gaping holes in them, and it's all good. I walk everywhere. Barefoot children come out to greet me with big smiles, I'm welcomed into homes, I have wonderful meals in the street, I talk to people as my friend translates, we do The Work. One man says he has seven bullet holes in his body; he shows me some of them and says he was shot for throwing rocks at Israeli soldiers. When he talks politics, he seethes with confusion and despair. He still believes that throwing rocks is the way to bring about change. Bullets haven't convinced him otherwise. That's the power of believing our insane thoughts.

I am free to walk anywhere in the world, with anyone, at any time. I can't project danger. There are no limitations to where I go. I love going, because I love what I travel with. Sanity doesn't suffer, ever. A clear mind is beautiful and sees only its own reflection. It bows in humility to itself; it falls at its own feet. It doesn't add anything or subtract anything; it simply knows the difference between what's real and what's not. And because of this, danger isn't a possibility.

A lover of what is looks forward to everything: life, death, disease, loss, earthquakes, bombs, anything the mind might be tempted to call "bad." Life will bring us everything we need, to show us what we haven't undone yet. Nothing outside ourselves can make us suffer. Except for our unquestioned thoughts, every place is paradise.

THE WORK IN ACTION

"My children shouldn't suffer."

SARAH: *I need to protect my children, or else something bad will happen to them.*

KATIE: "You need to protect your children"—**is that true?**

SARAH: Logically, I know this is ridiculous, because they're all grown up, and they have their own lives, and they're very capable adults, with children of their own. But it's almost like an instinctual drive. I feel I need to protect them.

KATIE: Yes, sweetheart, and is your answer yes or no?

SARAH: It's yes. But I don't *want* to do this to myself or my children anymore. It's hard.

KATIE: I hear that you *do* want to protect your children.

SARAH: Right. Correct.

KATIE: Okay, so we're getting it down to what's true for you. "I don't want to take care of them anymore. They don't like me doing it, I'm exhausted, I don't want to do that anymore"—**is that true?** No. [The audience laughs.]

SARAH: No.

KATIE: "You need to protect your children"—**can you absolutely know that that's true?**

SARAH [after a pause]: No, I can't know that. I can't know that that's what I really need.

KATIE: Good, sweetheart. That's major. That's a major thing to realize for yourself. **How do you react when you believe that thought?** How do you react when you believe that you need to protect your children, and in reality they're perfectly fine without your protection? That's the proof. And watch your mind think, "Yeah, but . . ." How do you react when you believe the thought "I need to protect my children" and they don't want your help or you can't get to them or you aren't able to help them when you believe they need it?

SARAH: I tighten up. I worry about them all the time.

KATIE: And when you tighten up and worry, how do you treat your children? Follow it out.

SARAH: I guess I'm overprotective.

KATIE: I would drop the "I guess." [The audience laughs.] What do you do specifically?

SARAH: Well, I give them advice all the time. I try to get them to be careful, not to take risks. When they're having a good time, I'm one step ahead and worrying about what may come next. I try to control their lives. Sometimes I'm not a lot of fun.

KATIE: Oh, honey. **Who would you be without the thought?** Who would you be if you didn't have the ability to think the thought "I need to protect them"?

SARAH [after a pause]: I'd be a lot less anxious. I'd be a woman living her own life and letting her children live theirs. I'd be someone who doesn't think she needs to control the world for her children to be safe. I'd be happy.

KATIE: Now turn the thought around. "You need to protect your children"—**turn it around.**

SARAH: I *don't* need to protect my children.

KATIE: Is that as true or truer?

SARAH: It's truer. I can see that. But Katie, I don't want them to suffer. This goes so deep.

KATIE: You don't want them to suffer. Why not?

SARAH: Doesn't every mother feel that? I just want them to be happy.

KATIE: Why don't you want them to suffer? When they suffer, what happens to *you*?

SARAH: I suffer, too.

KATIE: *You* suffer. Isn't that why you don't want *them* to suffer? It's important to really get that straight.

SARAH: I *don't* have it straight. Seeing one of my children suffering is worse than me suffering.

KATIE: It would have to be worse, because you're projecting what they're going through. You're projecting your own feelings onto them. It's your own feelings that are hurting you, not their pain.

SARAH [after a pause]: That's true.

KATIE: And when you're doing that, who is going through it? Who is suffering? You are.

SARAH: Mmm.

KATIE: So you look at their suffering, and you project that it's, let's say, six or seven on a scale of one to ten, and for all you know it's only a one, and your suffering about their suffering is a seven.

SARAH: Could be.

KATIE: Here's something I often say: What I love about separate bodies is that when you hurt, I don't. It's not my turn. And when I do hurt, I'm going to be honest about it. I hurt. Look at the tears in my eyes—this is my pain, not yours. You're free of pain right now, free also to help me if you can. If you're projecting my pain and experiencing it as yours, how can you be available to help? And when *you* hurt, I don't have to do that.

SARAH: How did you stop doing that?

KATIE: I did The Work. I questioned my mind. I was tired of the pain, and I'm fascinated at how free the mind can get. The freer you get, the more you love yourself. And self-love loves everything it sees. That's all it has to project out onto the world. "Love thy neighbor as thyself." I always have: I hated me, I hated you. Today I love me, and there is nothing I can do not to love you. That's how it works. Now think of the worst time in your life, the worst thing you ever suffered.

SARAH: Okay.

KATIE: You got through it, didn't you?

SARAH: Sure. It was hard, but I got through it.

KATIE: Okay. So who do you think you are to believe that *they* can't get through it? If you can do it, why would you believe that they can't get through whatever difficulties life hands them?

SARAH: I see that.

KATIE: Yes, sweetheart. You got through yours, so what leads you to believe that they aren't at least as capable and courageous as you are? What leads you to believe that they have fewer survival skills than you do?

SARAH: What occurs to me right now is that they didn't when they were little.

KATIE: Really? That's a good one. "They didn't have those survival skills when they were little"—**turn it around.** "I didn't . . ."

SARAH: True. I didn't have the survival skills . . .

KATIE: ". . . when they . . ."

SARAH: When they were little.

KATIE: Yes. The fearless, creative "you" didn't survive. I've watched children, I've seen how fearless they are before we teach them fear. I'm still learning survival skills from them. When they bump into a door, they don't look around to see who saw them. [The audience laughs.] I'm learning survival skills from my two- and three-year-old grandchildren. And I learn from my grown children as well. I watch as they go through the problems in their lives, amazingly—can you believe it?—without my help. But that's because I've sat back and watched. I want to know my children. And if I'm in there trying to fix everything, I can't know that they have survival skills, because I'm always stepping in before I can find out. And they don't need the skills because I'm always there! That's what we teach when we keep stepping in before we're asked.

SARAH: I can see that.

KATIE: So the reason you don't want your children to suffer is because you suffer when they do. It's all about you. Now what would happen if those children weren't there, if something happened to them? Suppose they were in a constant state of pain, and the doctors said, "There's nothing we can do about it," and there's no euthanasia that's legal.

SARAH: That's my worst nightmare.

KATIE: Yes, that's where the unquestioned mind goes. "My children are going to suffer forever, and there's nothing I can do about it." And then you're left with yourself and your suffering, because it's out of your control. And that will leave you yourself to deal with. That's why I like to deal with it *before* life happens. That way, I'm prepared for life, and I can be of much more help. It's so much more efficient. I'm here to do what I can, not what I can't and what is unnecessary.

SARAH: Yes, I can see that.

KATIE: When another person suffers, there's nothing I can do about that, except maybe to put my arms around them or bring them a cup of tea and let them know that I'm totally available. But that's where it must end. The rest is up to them. And because I made it through, I know that they can do it. I am *not* special.

SARAH: This is so deep.

KATIE: Life will test you. So when they're suffering, and there's no euthanasia that's legal, and you don't want to go to jail for murder, and the doctor says they're in pain for the rest of their lives—

twenty more years, let's say, or fifty more years—there's nothing you can do. Every doctor says there's nothing that can be done, that's how it is, they're in terrible pain. "You wouldn't be able to handle it"—**is that true?**

SARAH: Boy, it sure feels true.

KATIE: And I'm asking you to look deeper. Let's check into a little reality here! "You wouldn't be able to handle it"—**can you absolutely know that that's true?**

SARAH [after a long pause]: No, I can't absolutely know that. For all I know, maybe I *would* be able to handle it.

KATIE: Of course you'd handle it! There's no one in this room that wouldn't be able to handle it. That's how it is. You'd stand there suffering over their suffering, and then you'd have to go to the bathroom. And on the way back from the bathroom, you'd see something or smell something and just for that one moment you'd forget that your children were suffering. Then you'd get hungry. Then you'd eat, and maybe you'd enjoy your food, and maybe you'd feel guilty for enjoying your food. Then you'd get bored with the hospital room. "I need some fresh air!" And you'd make some excuse about getting out, and you'd think that you're a terrible mother for leaving the room . . . as you're dying to get out. And then you'd think that the couch in the hospital room isn't quite as comfortable as the one at home, and eventually you'd go home, and then you'd go to sleep. One way or another, you'd handle it.

SARAH: That sounds true. It's true to my experience.

KATIE: **How do you react when you believe the thought** "I couldn't handle it"? How do you react when you believe this lie? And I'm calling it a lie because you yourself said that it's not true, that you can't know that it's true.

SARAH: My throat constricts, I feel heavy in my chest and my gut. And I fantasize about the more terrible things that are going to happen after this.

KATIE: Exactly. Your mind goes into the future, and it creates hell, it creates even more suffering than the apparent problem you're dealing with, as though that one were not enough. And then how do you treat . . . let's say it's your daughter. How do you treat your daughter, who is in such terrible pain? How do you treat your daughter when you believe the thought "I can't handle it"?

SARAH: I get terrified and overwhelmed. I pull away from her. My own pain feels so overwhelming that I can't really be there for her.

KATIE: How do you deal with life when you believe the thought "I can't handle it"? We separate from it, don't we? "I just can't bear it! I can't bear to see her like this!" Well, that's your daughter. **Who would you be without the thought?**

SARAH: I would be much calmer. I'd be confident. I'd be able to look into her eyes and hold her hand, however terribly she was suffering.

KATIE: Yes, sweetheart, that would be truer to your nature. **Turn it around.**

SARAH: I *could* handle it.

KATIE: Yes. I could handle seeing her like this. I'm not the one in pain here! It's her. You're confused. It's all about you. Me, me, me, me, I, I, me, I. And then there's me, I, I, I, me. "*I* can't handle it!"—as your daughter lies dying. And your heart is shut down. And we wonder why we're so separate from life. It's because we believe thoughts like "I can't handle it," and all the time we can.

SARAH: Oh, my! That is so amazing. I never understood that before.

KATIE: To wake up to reality is to amaze yourself, to be amazed at your strength, your love, your devotion. **Who would you be** in the presence of that child **without the thought** "I can't handle it"?

SARAH: I would be alert and present, I think.

KATIE: I think so, too. And I have been tested. I know what it is to be fully present with a suffering child or a dying mother. There's no separation in it, because I don't believe the thought "I can't handle it." I'm so intimate with them. If they're going to die, I don't want to miss a single moment with them. But the thought "I can't handle it" keeps us separate. We have them dead in our minds, and they're still living.

SARAH: I *can* handle it.

KATIE: It's good to get a grip on reality. A mother's grip on reality is a wonderful thing.

SARAH: Thank you so much, Katie. I can't tell you how helpful this is.

KATIE: You're so welcome. I love that you've realized you can handle anything life brings you. It gives your children a break. It certainly gives you one. And it gives you a clear example of the power of love.

36

If you want to get rid of something,
you must first allow it to flourish.

I've come to see that there is no such thing as criticism, there are only observations. And there is no observation that does not enlighten me, if my mind is open to it. What could anyone say to me that I couldn't agree with? If someone tells me I'm a terrible person, I go inside myself, and in two seconds I can find where in my life I've been a terrible person; it doesn't take much searching. And if someone says I'm a wonderful person, I can easily find that, too. This is about self-realization, not about right or wrong. It's about freedom.

When someone tells me that I lied, for example, I go inside to see if they're right. If I can't find it in the situation they've mentioned, I can easily find it in some other situation, maybe decades ago. I don't say that out loud. But inside me, it's a joining. And then I can say, "I *am* a liar. I see where you're right about me." We agree. That person is realizing who I used to be, the very thing that I began realizing twenty years ago. I fall in love with people who are angry at me. They're like people suffering on their deathbeds: we don't kick them and say, "Get up." It's the same when someone is angry and attacking you. This is a confused human being. And if I'm clear, where is it that I couldn't meet him? That's when we are the happiest, when we're giving ourselves without condition.

I have a good deal of practice at this. Paul, my ex-husband, used to yell at me a lot, especially after I got a little clarity in 1986. He wasn't happy with my change. He would just wail through the house, yelling, "Who are you, Goddamn it? Where's the woman I married? What did you do with her? You don't love me. If you loved me, you'd stay at home and not travel. You love everybody else as much as you love me." And of course he was right, from his point of view. He equated loving him with doing what he wanted me to do, and his story overrode reality every time. When he yelled at me, his chest and face would expand, he'd blow up like a balloon, get very red and very loud, and wave his arms a lot. All I could see was a dear man who was frightened of losing me and who was doing the best he could. He was yelling at himself, thinking it was me. And I would just love him and appreciate him and listen to the music of his complaints, as his imagination created the wife who didn't care, and moved farther and farther away from reality, so far that the distance seemed unbridgeable. Finally, in his hurt and anger, he would turn away from me as if I didn't exist. And I didn't.

If a criticism hurts you, that means you're defending against it. Your body will let you know very clearly when you're feeling hurt or defensive. If you don't pay attention, the feeling rises and becomes anger and attack, in the form of defense or justification. It's not right or wrong; it just isn't intelligent. War is not intelligent. It doesn't work. If you're really interested in your own peace of mind, you'll become more and more aware of that sense of wanting to defend yourself against a criticism. And eventually you'll be fascinated to find the missing pieces of yourself that your critic is helpfully pointing out, and you'll ask him to tell you more, so that you can be enlightened even further.

Criticism is an immense gift for those who are interested in self-realization. For those who aren't, welcome to hell, welcome to being at war with your partner, your neighbors, your children, your boss. When you open your arms to criticism, you are your own direct path to freedom, because you can't change us or what we think about you. You are your only way to stand with a friend as a friend, even when she perceives you as an enemy. And until you can be intimate with us however badly we think of you, your Work isn't done.

After you've done inquiry for a while, you can listen to any criticism without defense or justification, openly, delightedly. It's the end of trying to control what can't ever be controlled: other people's perception. The mind rests, and life becomes kinder, and then totally kind, even in the midst of apparent turmoil. When you're aware of being a student, everyone in the world becomes your teacher. In the absence of defensiveness, gratitude is all that's left.

37

The Tao never does anything,
yet through it all things are done.

Try to make yourself do nothing. You can't. You're being breathed, being thought, being moved, being lived. There's nothing you can do not to eat when it's time to eat, or sleep when it's time to sleep. If you just watch, allowing whatever comes to come and whatever goes to go, you can realize in every moment that you don't need anything but what you have.

Where are your hands right now? Who put them there? Did *you* do that? And then, no matter what your thinking is, you—it—moved again. Maybe it moved your foot. Maybe it swallowed, or it blinked your eyes. Just notice. That's how you enter not-doing, where everything falls sweetly into place.

The miraculous life of not-doing has an intelligence of its own. I realize that I'm not doing anything, and in that awareness the fullness that's always present is recognized. I may find myself humming or smiling as things simply get done. And an opposite that's equally beautiful must mirror the fullness; God must mirror God. The experience is joy without personality or investment, watching out of eyes unknown.

Not my words, not my presence, nothing about me is of value to other people. What is of value can't be seen or heard. I'm invisible.

But what people *can* see, through inquiry, is their own truth. That's where the value is; that's what can be experienced when you're tired of suffering. You can reach out and have that, because it is your very own. Whenever it seems personal, as if I'm the one who has it, it can't be accepted, because there *is* nothing personal, and people know this deep inside. You can take the four questions and find yourself. The questions are the path back to your self. They don't care what the story is. They just wait for you to answer them.

38

The Master doesn't try to be powerful,
thus she is truly powerful.

The Master doesn't try to be powerful, because she realizes how unnecessary that is. Power doesn't need a plan. Everything gravitates to it. With each moment, new options are born. It's like a Fourth of July sparkler: you light it with a match, and sparks fly. Each moment is like that, a new opportunity to be used. If someone says no, the Master sees options as the sparks flying from its center. The no opens the door for something that couldn't have been foreseen. Here is a way, and there is a way. Each way comes from the Master's openness to possibilities. In seeing the wisdom of the no, she keeps the door open for something better.

I never have the sense that anything I haven't done is undone. I see the things that don't get done as things that need a different timing; I and the world are better off without them, for now. I have hundreds of e-mails waiting for me on my computer, some of them from people who are desperately asking for my response, but I never feel frustrated that I don't have time to answer them. I do the best I can, and I'm clear that people don't need me; since we all come from the same wisdom, they can give themselves what they need if I'm not available. What really matters is always available to everyone. Nothing comes ahead of its time, and nothing has ever happened that didn't need to happen.

Bringing inquiry to people is my job. After that, there's nothing to offer. I know that ultimately people don't need my help. I go through the world helping people, it appears, and I'm only selfishly helping myself. When you say, "Help me," I understand that. I've been there. But even if I could give you freedom, I wouldn't do it. I love you too much for that. I leave your freedom to you. That's the gift.

My job is to delete myself. If there were a bumper sticker representing my life, it would say CTRL-ALT-DELETE: www.thework.com. That's where I invite everyone to come join me. Join me and delete your own beautiful self. That's the only place where we *can* meet. I call it love.

39

The Master views the parts with compassion,
because she understands the whole.
Her constant practice is humility.

The voice within is what I honor. It's what I'm married to. This life
doesn't belong to me. The voice says, "Do the dishes"—okay.
I don't know what it's for, I just do it. If I don't follow the order, that's
all right, too. But this is a game about where life will take me when I
do follow. There's nothing more exciting than to say yes to such a
wild thing. I don't have anything to lose. I can afford to be a fool.

What fun is it to be God if I can't get a glimpse of myself in the
mirror? And whether I like it or not, that's what I am. I'm vanity—
total vanity. So when people are attached to their looks and their
health, it's coming from an honest source; it's just misdirected. It's
pure innocence.

The ego—mind projected as a body, as a you—is nothing more
than a mirror image thinking that it's God and misinterpreting the
world. It's the mirror image thinking that it's the source, misinterpreting It as itself, rather than itself as just a reflection of It. It's under the
painful illusion that it's separate. But the truth is that the ego goes
where God goes. God—reality—is all of it. The ego has no options. It
can protest all it wants, but if God moves, *it* moves.

When someone says that the world is a terrible place, he becomes the champion of suffering, projecting that there's something wrong here, something less than beautiful. It's the mirror image without a clue that it's just a mirror image. You are the *is,* the reflection, the storyless movement. As soon as you realize that, the source is merged with; the reflection moves, without argument, as the source. And that is simple awareness, the joy of what people call the world and what I refer to as the image of God itself dancing.

Humility is what happens when you're caught and exposed to yourself, and you realize that you're no one and you've been trying to be someone. You just die and die into the truth of that. You die into what you have done and who you have been, and it's a very sweet thing; there's no guilt or shame in it. You become totally vulnerable, like a little child. Defense and justification keep falling away, and you die into the brilliance of what is real.

As I noticed the falling-away of the self and saw that its construct was absolutely invalid, what remained was humbled through the recognition. Everything dissolved—all that I had imagined myself to be. I realized that I was none of it, that everything I'd stood for was insubstantial and ridiculous. And what remained from that fell away, too, until finally there was nothing left to be humble about, no one left to be humble. If I was anything, I was gratitude. As the circle comes to a close in this way, it's difficult to tell whether the feeling is humility or gratitude. Names no longer fit.

Gratitude, you could say, is what remains of the experience of humility. That's my favorite position. It's a sense of kissing the ground, *licking* the ground for its pure deliciousness, kissing the feet of the master that is everything without exception. There is such a sense of thankfulness for no longer being the person who thinks she knows and who has to live life out of that limited, claustrophobic mind. And of course I am that person as well. I remember when I believed those thoughts, so I have a reference, I understand how others see it. I watch their confusion with nothing but love, because they're innocent children who feel that something's askew, yet keep moving toward the polarity that never works, where they want to win, to do it right, to do more, to have more, to plan, to defend, to protect, to be loved, to be admired, and to undergo the shame of settling for less than their heart's desire.

40

Return is the movement of the Tao.
Yielding is the way of the Tao.

You can't have it, because you already *are* it. You already have what you want, you already are what you want. That's as good as it gets. It appears as this now—perfect, flawless. And to argue with it is to experience a lie. The Work can give you this wonderful awareness: the awareness of the lie and of the power of truth, the beauty of what really is.

The four questions unravel each story, and the turnaround leads back to the storyteller: you. You are the storyteller. You have become the stories you told yourself. And you are what lives prior to every story. Every story, every thing, is God: reality. It apparently emerges from out of itself, and it appears as a life. It lives forever within the story, until the story ends. From out of itself, I appeared as my story, until the questions brought me home. I love it that inquiry is so unfailing. Story: suffering. Inquiry: no story (no suffering). Freedom is possible in every moment.

When I say things like "Until I'm free to be happy in the presence of my greatest enemy, my work's not done," people can hear that as a motive for doing inquiry. It's not; it's an observation. If you do The Work with any kind of motive, even the best of motives—getting your husband back or healing your body or saving the world—it won't be genuine, because you'll be looking for a certain kind of answer, and you won't allow the deeper answers to surface. Only when you don't know what you're looking for can you be open to the answers that will change your life. Any motive other than the love of truth won't work. It's the truth that sets you free. That's an accurate statement—it's not just written in a bible somewhere. And the truth we're talking about is not someone else's truth; it's your own. That's the only truth that can set you free.

Yielding or surrendering to the way of it is easy once your mind is clear. What people call surrender is actually a noticing. You notice that everything is continually disappearing, and you celebrate it as it goes back to where it came from: non-existence, the uncreated. And eventually surrender ceases to be necessary. The word implies that there's something outside you to surrender to. But you just notice what isn't, what's gone, what you can never prove existed in the first place—a sound, a name, a picture, a voice. You keep noticing, until finally there's nothing to surrender to.

The mind surrenders to itself. When it isn't at war with itself, it experiences a world that is completely kind, the benevolent mind projecting a benevolent world. It can no longer validate suffering on this earth, because it has ended suffering within itself. It becomes completely pitiless, completely loving.

People ask how I can live if nothing has meaning and I'm no one. It's simple. We're being lived. We're not doing it. Without a story, we move effortlessly, fluidly, without resistance. This possibility can be very frightening for people who think that they have control. So question your thoughts, and see how life goes on so much more kindly without you. Even in the world's apparent collapsing, I see only joy.

If you knew how important you are, you would fragment into a billion pieces and just be light. Any concept keeps you from the awareness of that. If you really knew who you are without your story, you'd have to be the nameless, the limitless, the ecstatic—just a fool, crazy with love. It's so painful to live outside the light. I don't know how people do it. It was so painful that I could do it for only forty-three years. (Forty-three centuries.)

41

The direct path seems long.

The direct path might seem long, because mind tells you of a distance and mesmerizes you with its proof. When you believe that thought, you feel the exhaustion that accompanies it, the heaviness, the stress. But the direct path isn't long. In fact, there's no distance to it at all. Where are you going, other than where you are right now? How can you go anywhere else? The direct path means realizing that the beginning and end of every journey is where you always are.

You can't make a decision. You can only experience a story about how you made it. Decisions make themselves; they're happenings; they come when the time is right. I like to ask, "Are you breathing yourself?" No? Well, maybe you're not thinking yourself or making decisions, either. Maybe reality doesn't move until it moves, like a breath, like the wind. And when you tell the story of how you're doing it, you keep yourself from the awareness that you are nature, flowing perfectly. Who would you be without the story that you need to make a decision? If it's your integrity to make a decision, make it. And guess what? In five minutes, you might change your mind and call it "you" again.

I love how mind changes. I watch it and am steadfast in that delight. I love the sweet movement and flavor of mind changing. I move as it moves, without an atom of resistance. It shifts like the wind. I say yes, because there is no reason to say no, and I say no very easily, too. No is as effortless as yes. I say whatever I know is true for me. It sometimes confuses people; they misunderstand, and they do what they need to do with it. And I am very clear that a no is as loving as a yes, because I am always saying yes to my integrity. A no is a yes, too, when it comes from integrity.

Mind changes constantly, it seems, and never changes at all. I'm rooted in what can't change. Wherever you come from, I'll come from that same position in order to meet you. That's why some of the things I say appear to be contradictory. At different times I'm coming from different directions, and they're all true. Every direction is equal. It can sound inconsistent or like a puppy chasing its tail: it seems to go nowhere. It can sound like someone speaking in riddles. It can be confusing, and from one vantage point it can't be followed. Someone who's doing The Work with me may not hear the contradiction at all, because we are so intimately joined in the moment, whereas to a person in the audience it may sound like gibberish. But if you listen without thinking about what I mean, if you just immerse yourself in the experience of it, going inside and answering the questions for yourself rather than waiting for the other person to answer, you won't hear it as gibberish. It will make perfect sense.

When I'm working with someone, I don't think about the outcome. I'm not concerned with whether you're taking it in, or how deep your insight is, or what you do with it or how far you go with it, or whether you're in total resistance or have a major awakening. What I care about is what you care about. If your answers are shallow and limited, that's all right with me, because I see that it's all the depth that's required in your world right now. If you seem to make no headway whatsoever, I understand that the illusion you're holding on to is precious for you, and if you want to keep it, that's what I want. Or if, on the contrary, the bottom falls out as you're answering the questions, and everything you thought you knew drops away, and you fall into the abyss of reality, I love that you've given that to yourself;

I love the polarity you've entered, the don't-know mind, where every-thing is surprising, fresh, and brilliant, and you're like a child discovering life for the first time. But that isn't my preference unless it's yours. Why would I want to take your world from you, even if I could? Nothing comes ahead of its time.

We're all children, even the wisest of us. We're all five-year-olds, just learning how to do this thing called life. When someone calls me wise, I laugh at the thought of living so small. Infinite mind always leaps ahead of itself, leaving the world in the dust. It always exceeds its own genius. It's a child, and it's ageless. It lives in the unknown, it thrives on the unknown. That's its nourishment and its delight. That's the place where its creative power is free.

A retarded man comes up to me as I sign books after a reading at a bookstore. He has a huge waist and a small, almost conical head, his tongue is hanging out of his mouth like a dog's, his hands and his arms flail around, his eyes wander. I can't help falling in love with him, his authenticity, the beautiful way of it. It's clear that he wants me to come close to him. I'm being invited into his world. "Hello," he says. "My name is Bob." He speaks very slowly, slurs his words, drools. I accept the invitation and move close to him, we put our foreheads together. His eyes meet mine, then dart here and there; I look straight into them and wait for them to return. And out of nowhere his arms reach around me and pull my cheek to his lips, and he kisses me with a small grunting sound. There are no words for this generosity. The moment goes on and on. He seems to know what I know: that he is the light of my life, my world, my everything. I look into his eyes, then say, "Thank you for the kiss." And I notice how adequate my thank-you is. The experience of love is vast and all-consuming; how could a simple thank-you be enough? Yet it is. Even when you're totally consumed by love, "Thank you" is all that's necessary.

How am I going to leave the love of my life? I hear myself say, "Good-bye, Bob. I love you." And I notice life entering me as I walk away—the people, the walls, the doorway. Life continues to flow into me just as that dear man flowed in. Every step is where I am, even though it appears that I'm moving. How wonderful not to need the world, not to go out toward it, but always to allow it to meet and enter me. I find that there's room in me for everything, everyone, every situation, every flavor of being. I love the openness that I am.

42

Ordinary people hate solitude.
But the Master makes use of it,
embracing her aloneness, realizing
she is one with the whole universe.

We're born alone, we die alone, and we live alone, each on our own planet of perception. No two people have ever met. Even the people you know best and love with all your heart are your own projections. Sooner or later, you're the one who's left. Do you realize how wonderful that is? After all, you're the one you go to sleep with and wake up with, you're the one who orders your favorite food and loves your favorite music. You've always been your favorite subject— your *only* subject. It's all about you.

There's nothing sweeter than being with myself, by myself. The amusement, the wonder of thoughts! They appear so real in their brilliance, they create the whole world, the majesty and play of it, the life of feelings, the joys that mind brings forth as nectar to itself. Thoughts appear from nowhere, they move by like clouds, they change, they dissipate, they're gone. Who named the sky? How did he know that?

I sit with my eyes closed. Two hours pass, then it occurs to me that not a single thought has happened. I discover that tears of joy are running down my cheeks. I don't stop them, even though the joy seems bigger than I can contain. All that it is, all that it was and ever could be, is invited to live at its highest power, now. It's all right if it kills me; it doesn't matter, I know not to stop it. I become so bright, so weightless and lived, so fearlessly allowing, that the joy can have its own full life through me. And as everything becomes visible, I see its true nature, which is love. Everything else is burned up as this joy has its way with me. I could kiss the ground, I could make love with the dirt, with the cement, the leaves, the soil, the texture of reality between fingers that can't even hold it. There's nothing to grasp, nothing that can be controlled. I notice that I'm worshiping not with any words, but with palm of hand against cheek. Where will this love end? How could I possibly know? And, eventually, the sobbing changes to the softest whisper, a breath, and then not even that.

43

The gentlest thing in the world
overcomes the hardest thing in the world.

The gentlest thing in the world is an open mind. Since it doesn't believe what it thinks, it is flexible, porous, without opposition, without defense. Nothing has power over it. Nothing can resist it. Even the hardest thing in the world—a closed mind—can't resist the power of openness. Ultimately the truth flows into it and through it, like water through rock.

When the mind first becomes a student of itself, it learns that nothing in the world can possibly oppose it: everything is for it, everything adds to it, enlightens it, nourishes it, reveals it. It continues to open, because it's in a fearless, undefended state, and it's hungry for knowledge. And when it realizes that it's nothing, it can penetrate everywhere, even when there's no room for it, no place to receive it.

People are afraid to be nothing. But being nothing is only one aspect of it. Not only is it nothing to be afraid of, it's a cause for celebration. Without your stressful story, there is no stress—obviously! When you don't believe your thoughts, there's only laughter and peace. There are names for a place like that. I call it heaven. And how can people know what nothingness is while they still believe what they think? "Something is better than nothing"—can you absolutely know that that's true?

The truly open mind doesn't have a goal or a purpose other than to be what it is. It's not attached to concepts of self or other. It realizes that ultimately there are no humans, there is no mind. When the mind opens, you lose everything, gratefully. I'm sitting here as a woman, and in the next realization I'm a galaxy or an ant. It doesn't matter. You lose everything, and then there's the reentry. On a good-hair day, don't you love to look in the mirror? That's what it's like. You're looking in the mirror at nothing, delighted. When you're nothing, it's always a good-hair day.

I can't know what the world is going to be. My body is never the same twice. It's tired, it's rested, it's large, then immediately it's thin. I can never recognize it. I see it as old, and that's lovely. And then it shifts before my eyes again and becomes the body of a young girl. It's like glimpsing something, and then you look again and it wasn't that at all. It's absolutely gorgeous, then it shifts to something unfathomable. I don't know what it is or whose it is or why it is. And what it does is fascinating. Its own hand begins stroking its own leg, for no reason other than to apply lotion to skin that doesn't need it. And then it will hold a cup of anything and drink it, a liquid I call tea, for example, but I can never know that, either. My world is one of constantly shifting forms. There's nothing I can count on in it, not my age, not my body, not who is with me, not my identity, not the century, not the planet I live on.

Mind appears, if it appears, only to end itself. The projected world goes first, then the mind that projected it. No trace of it remains. Silence is all that's possible—the openness of never having existed in the first place. That's where I live. When it's over, it's over. You can't create or uncreate it. You wouldn't want to.

44

When you realize that there is nothing lacking,
the whole world belongs to you.

Success is the story of having arrived somewhere, on your way from an imagined past to an imagined future. I don't even have a reference for it. For me, whatever I'm doing is a success—the ultimate success. The whole world belongs to me, because I live in the simplicity of what is: woman sitting in chair. There's nothing beyond this, not one thought beyond it. This room *is* the whole world. I'm a success at sitting. I'm a success at breathing. If I died now, I'd be a success at *not* breathing. What could I possibly fail at? When the mind is clear, there's no way to make a mistake.

Reality is kind. Its nature is uninterrupted joy. When I woke up from the dream of Byron Katie, there was nothing left, and the nothing was benevolent. It's so benevolent that it wouldn't reappear, it wouldn't re-create itself. The worst thing could happen, the worst imagination of horror, the whole planet could be obliterated, and it would see that as grace, it would even celebrate, it would open its arms and sing "Halleluyah!" It's so clear, so in love with what is, that it might seem unkind, even inhuman. It cares totally, and it doesn't care at all, not one bit, not if all living creatures in the universe were obliterated in an instant. How could it react with anything less than joy? It's in love with what is, whatever form that may take.

Reality is neither good nor bad. It's bigger than good and bad. It has no opposite, there's nothing that it's not, there's nothing that isn't like it. The end of duality isn't the end of the world: it's the end of suffering. The brilliant, the bright—that's what I'd call God if I called it anything. What doesn't exist, what is beyond existence, is more brilliant than the sun. During one of my weekend intensives, a man once said to me, with the loveliest glow on his face, "I just understood! It's amazing: what you're talking about is heaven on earth!" I said, "You do understand. And actually, I'm talking *from* heaven, to earth." (I love my little jokes.)

As you begin to wake yourself up from your dreams of hell or purgatory, heaven dawns on you in a way that the imagination can't comprehend. And then, as you continue to question what you believe, you realize that heaven, too, is just a beginning. There is something better than heaven. It's the eternal, meaningless, infinitely creative mind. It can't stop for time or space or even joy. It's so brilliant that it will shake what's left of you into the depths of all-consuming wonder.

I can't find anything outside the brilliance. It's everywhere, and it's always gone, even before it happens. It's how form appears to take place. And by the time form happens, original cause is already gone, so the taste, smell, or sight is gone even as it appears to be happening, and mind is so delighted that it never experiences the effects. Wouldn't you be delighted, too, if you knew the secret of life, the cosmic joke that's going on all the time? The joke is that there's nothing. You see that all stressful thoughts are already gone, you realize that there's no substance to them, and you feel intense delight. Then you see that all beautiful things, all the things you love, all the great art and music and literature, all the people you love most dearly, our whole civilization, the beloved earth itself, the whole infinite universe, are gone as well, and you smile with triple delight, because you realize that not only are they not real, you're not real, either.

45

True perfection seems imperfect,
yet it is perfectly itself.

Perfection is another name for reality. The only way you can see anything as imperfect is if you believe a thought about it. "It's inadequate, it's ugly, it's unfair, it's flawed"—is that true? This chipped coffee cup on the table: how beautiful it is when you simply look at it, without any thought of what it should be. Or the homeless man shuffling ahead of you on the sidewalk, with long brown stains down the legs of his jeans. Or the wars and killings and bombings that you read about on the front page of the newspaper. When you see that reality is perfect just as it is, you can only stand in awe at the brilliant, unceasing, relentless way of it.

My legs are on the coffee table, crossed at the ankles. One person might think, *How unladylike;* another might think, *How comfortable.* But with or without the thoughts, my legs are in the perfect position. And then I notice that they uncross, and then they cross again, as I watch the movie of life, frame by frame: perfection, perfection, perfection, perfection. There is no frame you could freeze and look at that wouldn't be the way of its perfect self. Only the mind that believes what it thinks is capable of creating imperfection.

What could happen that wouldn't be good? My legs cross, they uncross, they stretch, they fold. Usually they're comfortable; sometimes they're so restless that they have to stand up and move. It's all good. Everything that happens is God's will. When you realize that, you're home free.

I'm wide open to discomfort, blindness, injury, death. Just this morning, I missed a step because I couldn't see it, and I almost fell down a flight of stairs. I watched myself catch my balance, fascinated. It was like being on a roller coaster with one of my grandsons. What a trip! "I need to live"—can I absolutely know that that's true? I took a drink of water one day, and it went down what people call "the wrong pipe"—that is, it went down the right pipe even though people say it's wrong. I was breathing water, not air, and because I didn't believe the story that it was supposed to be air, there was no problem. Because I didn't have the concept "I need to breathe," I was a fish for a moment or two. The water went down, then it came up. It was very gentle, as if my lungs were being rinsed. But if I had believed the concept "I need to breathe," it could have been stressful. So we really are amphibious. We can't breathe water for long, but we can when we need to. No story: no resistance. The story is what we resist, not the experience. How do I know that the water was supposed to go down this pipe? That's where it went.

The insight that everything is God's will is not the end of the discussion for most people, but the beginning. Even devout people have trouble realizing that whatever happens is a good thing. They think that that's an oversimplification. But how can the simple truth be *too* simple? "God is everything, God is good" isn't an idea; it's reality. You can know that it's true because anything that opposes it hurts. I call it the last story. Keep it and have a wonderful life. And if you want to go deeper, even that story isn't true.

Being empty means that there are no obstacles in my mind to keep me from loving what is, whatever it is. The clear mind is absolutely still. Anything that comes into its awareness is a tilt, to be set straight again. It's always looking for something out of order, only to see the order. It makes sense of everything and rests in its unceasing awareness. Right now I am dictating to Stephen in a hotel room in East Berlin. He just took his right hand from the laptop keyboard and scratched his nose. I am stunned. I have no way to relate to what that is. I fully take it in, and I wait, and I see everything that it isn't: it's not a nose, not a face, not a man, not anything, and I see the beauty of that gesture, the amusement of it, and how it's equal to the hands on the keyboard again, and how both movements are nothing, and love flows out of that. It's all one unbroken flow. There's no me, there's no him, there's no separation. It isn't possible for this to be interrupted. It was shocking to see his hand on his nose, it's shocking to see his hands moving on the keyboard now. The way of it is so strange, it's like liquid geometry, always flowing into the right order. No matter what happens, the love flows out, nothing can interrupt it, no cry or scream or laughter; it's always at work, always recognizing, present, vigilant, meticulous. If you could understand how I see these two feet on the coffee table right now, you'd laugh until you fell helpless onto the floor. The seeing would kill everything but the pure joy of what sees.

What an amazing world the empty mind is! Everything fills it. Feet, legs, coffee table, nose, arms, hands, laptop, walls, floor, windows, curtains, all of them nameless and flowing into and out of one another. Imagine being filled with nothing, and the weirdness of that, and how only that could make sense. And imagine the nature of itself that would produce the unending flow of fullness, and the container that could hold absolutely everything. There are no limits to it. Reality pours into us, and that's how it expands, that's how it manifests its infinite abundance. If mind were a body, it would be as if the light were just shooting in, sparkles of the most brilliant light, and it flows into you as a body, and rather than coming out of any orifice, it's contained—for example, instead of shooting out your fingertips, the light would stop there and the fingertips would expand out at the same rate at which the light would fill the body.

So it's fullness without limits. It has to have a way out, and yet it stays in. Reality is never too big for the open mind. It's as vast as life, it's not separate, and it keeps watching for anything apparently new and includes it in its infinite expansion. It's all-inclusive, a limitless container, and there's nothing too much for it, nothing that's not welcome, nothing that it wouldn't or couldn't include.

There is a perfection beyond what the unquestioned mind can know. You can count on it to take you wherever you need to be, whenever you need to be there, and always exactly on time. When mind understands that it is just the reflection of the nameless intelligence that has created the whole apparent universe, it is filled with delight. It delights that it is everything, it delights that it is nothing, it delights that it is brilliantly kind and free of all identity, free to be its unlimited, unstoppable, unimaginable life, it dances in the light of its own understanding that nothing has ever happened, and that everything that has ever happened—everything that ever can happen—is good.

46

There is no greater illusion than fear.

We can only be afraid of what we believe we are—whatever there is in ourselves that we haven't met with understanding. If I thought you might see me as boring, for example, it would frighten me, because I haven't questioned that thought. So it's not people who frighten me, it's me that frightens me. That's my job, to frighten me, until I investigate this fear for myself. The worst that can happen is that I think you think about me what I think about myself. So I am sitting in a pool of me.

All fear is like this. It's caused by believing what you think—no more, no less. It's always the story of a future. If you want fear on purpose, get a plan. Fear is not possible when you've questioned your mind; it can be experienced only when the mind projects the story of a past into a future. The story of a past is what enables us to project a future. If we weren't attached to the story of a past, our future would be so bright, so free, that we wouldn't bother to project time. We would notice that we're already living in the future, and that it's always now.

One day, a few years ago, I was walking down what turned out to be a private driveway. I noticed that there was no exit, and as I did, some large dogs charged toward me, barking loudly. My thought was "I wonder if they'll bite me now." I couldn't project that they would, so there wasn't any fear. They ran up to me, they growled and bared their teeth, they stopped, they sniffed me, I waited and watched, and I noticed that life was very sweet, so far. And then they walked me back to the beginning of the driveway. *They* were happy, *I* was happy . . . It was a wonderful reunion.

"But Katie," someone might say, "isn't fear biological? Isn't it necessary for the fight-or-flight response? I can see not being afraid of a growling dog, but what if you were in an airplane that was going down—wouldn't you be very scared?" Here's my answer: "Does your body have a fight-or-flight response when you see a rope lying on the path ahead of you? Absolutely not—that would be crazy. Only if you imagine that the rope is a snake does your heart start pounding. It's your *thoughts* that scare you into fight-or-flight—not reality." Of course, I can't know what I would think or feel in a hypothetical situation. All I can say is that it's been a long time since I've been afraid. And I have been in some very interesting circumstances.

Living fearlessly is natural when you've questioned your thoughts. People ask me what that looks like today, and I sometimes tell the story of the birth of my granddaughter Marley. When Roxann went into labor, we were all there in the delivery room—I, Stephen, my son-in-law, Scott, and Scott's parents. Everything was going well, until suddenly the baby got stuck in the birth canal. She began to sink back into the womb, and her heart went into distress. The hospital was small, and on this night, at three in the morning, it was understaffed, the doctor had no qualified assistant, and there was a sense of panic in the room. He decided on a caesarean section, brusquely dismissed us, and wheeled Roxann into surgery. She was screaming, and no one would tell us anything, so we had reasons to believe that she and her baby were in serious trouble. Then the screams stopped. We could hear angry or panicked instructions at the end of the hall. An assistant from the emergency room ran toward me, asked me to call a number and tell the person who answered to come to the hospital immediately, then ran off without explaining what it was all about. After I made the call, I walked over to Scott's parents. When they saw me, they said, "Katie, will you pray with us?" The question surprised me. I didn't have a reference for prayer. I looked into their dear, tired, frightened eyes and thought, *There's nothing I need to ask for. I want whatever God wants.* But I joined them, of course. They took my hands, closed their eyes and prayed, and I stood there with them, loving them, knowing how painful it can be to want a particular outcome.

During this experience, there was no internal resistance, no fear. For me, reality is God. I can always trust that. I don't have to guess what God's will is. Whatever happens is God's will, whether my child and grandchild live or die, and therefore it's my will. So my prayer is already answered. I love Roxann with all my heart, and I would gladly have given my life to save hers, and that was not being called for. As it happened, the caesarean section went well, and both Roxann and Marley were fine.

There is another way. If I had believed such thoughts as "It's better for Roxann to live than to die," "My granddaughter should be born," or "The doctor should have been better prepared," I would have been very upset. I might have barged into the emergency room, making it even more difficult for the staff. There might have been anger, frustration, terror, prayers (the kind that attempt to manipulate what cannot be manipulated). These are a few of the ways we react when we believe what we think. It's what the war with reality often looks like, and it's not only insane, it's hopeless, and very painful. But when you question your mind, thoughts flow in and out and don't cause any stress, because you don't believe them. And you instantly realize that their opposites could be just as true. Reality shows you, in that peace of mind, that there are no problems, only solutions. You know, to your very depths, that whatever happens is what should be happening. If I lose my grandchild or my daughter, I lose what wasn't mine in the first place. It's a good thing. Either that, or God is a sadist, and that's not my experience.

I don't order God around. I don't presume to know whether life or death is better for me or for anyone I love. How can I know that? All I know is that God is everything and God is good. That's my story, and I'm sticking to it.

47

The Master arrives without leaving,
sees the light without looking,
achieves without doing a thing.

On my bedside table is a lamp I don't turn on, and an alarm clock I don't use. I'm on book tour, and this is reality's way, night after night, of supplying my needs beyond what I need.

I'm so grateful to hotels. They give me pillows, mattresses, sheets, everything I need for a good night's sleep. Everything is always taken care of, beyond what I think I want. There are windows. There are tissues. There's a notepad and a pen. There's a Gideon Bible, so dear to so many, which stays in the drawer. On my bedside table there's also a bottle of water for my morning tea. I prefer bottled to tap water. I buy it at a gas station or a grocery store or the little shop in the hotel. I look at the brands of bottled water, curious to see which one my hand will choose, and loving that I never can know until it actually picks up the bottle. I enjoy the trip from the cooler to the cash register. The cashier is a man or a woman, young or old, white or dark or Asian. We usually exchange a few words. It isn't a little thing. All my life I have been waiting to meet this person. I feel a surge of gratitude for my preferences. I love where they take me. I love my morning tea.

48

True mastery can be gained
by letting things go their own way.

The more closely I look at something, the more I begin to notice that I really don't know what it is. A name arises, and with it the silent *Is it true?*, surrounded by and emanating the laughter that comes from not knowing. " 'I am Byron Katie'—is it true?" And as the question dissolves each proof, I am left as nothing—in other words, as the woman sitting here. I was born now, on this couch in a hotel room, with no past other than imagination. How charming! How absurd!

Whatever I see is infused with the light of mind. And that light illuminates the one sitting on the couch now, awake and everywhere and timeless. It dissolves everything in its brilliance, until there is no one on the couch. What can live but the everlasting laughter? Let there be light, let there be world, since the world, as I understand it to be, is always born now, and now is where it always ends.

Things go their own sweet way, whether you let them or not. The rose blooms without your approval and dies without your consent. Even though you haven't issued directions, the streetcar rings its bell, the taxi stops to pick up a man in a gray suit. The world runs perfectly. It's all done without you. It's all done *for* you, whether or not you interfere. Even your interference is life living itself out through you. Life continually pours forth its gifts and lives itself out in its own sweet way. All you need to do is notice. That's true mastery.

49

The Master has no mind of her own.
She works with the mind of the people.

Freedom means living in kindness, *as* kindness. It means never having a moment of fear, anger, or sadness—living totally exposed, as a gift. There's nothing personal in it.

You don't need to let go or understand or forgive. Forgiveness is realizing that what you thought happened didn't. You realize that there was never anything to forgive, and that's what The Work makes evident. It has all just been a misunderstanding within you. When you can see that, someone else has to say, "Oh, you're so forgiving," because you wouldn't have a clue yourself. That's true forgiveness.

I love helping you see that. It's just a matter of making the obvious more obvious. I don't do anything but join you wherever you have attached to a belief, and the only reason I do The Work with you is that you think you need it. I don't have any such thought; I love you just the way you are. You are my internal life, so your asking is my asking. It's just me asking myself for my own freedom. That's self-love. It's perfectly greedy; it wants you to have everything. I am so melded into you that when you breathe, it's my breath; when you sit, it's me sitting. You'll say something, and I am absolutely there at that moment. It's as if I own you and you own me. Your voice is my voice, literally. And it doesn't have any meaning for me, so that, without prejudice or separation, I can join you wherever you are.

The Master has no mind of her own. All she has to work with is the mind of the people. The mind of the people is her mind, because it's the only part of mind that is still identified, still believed. The people have her old mind, the mind she survived. She's only working with her own unenlightenment, the spell she herself cast and is now awake to. She cast the spell, she woke up to it, and as she works with the people, they wake up, too, as her very own self. Their freedom is hers. To work with the mind of the people is her joy and her only life.

She is good to people who are good, because all she can see is goodness—she has no reference for anything else. So she's also good to people who apparently aren't good. She sees them as confused children who are having a very hard time. It's painful to be mean and selfish. She knows from experience what that feels like, and when she's kind to people who reach out to her, however "good" or "bad" they have been, it's herself she is being kind to. She acts as a kindness to herself. For her, it's always goodness meeting goodness, the steady, unbroken flow of her own nature.

She trusts people who are untrustworthy, as she trusts people who are trustworthy. She trusts them all, completely, to do what they do. And since they always do exactly that, she can never be disappointed. People do what they do—she can depend on that. It's good that this one told the truth; look at the gifts that came out of that. It's good that that one lied; look at the gifts that came out of that. And because the Master understands that truthfulness is the key to her own heart, she is delighted when anyone else comes to realize it.

My friend said that he'd meet me at the restaurant at 7:00 p.m., and he's not here. I walk in anyway, sit down, wait for fifteen minutes, then order a meal. I notice that the waiters keep their commitment, they wait on me. The meal is wonderful. I don't wonder where he is, because I know that wherever he is, that's where he's supposed to be. There's nothing out of order. I'm not worried about him or annoyed that he's late, I haven't been thinking of him at all, I don't need to bother; all my thoughts return to the source they came from. The waiter is slow in bringing the check, and that's how I'm detained long enough to see my friend rushing to the table. Perfect timing! He sits down beside me, breathless, and proceeds to tell me his story. What could be better than one meal? Two: one for me and one for him. Good that he broke his word. Good that he wasn't trustworthy. What could be more fulfilling than that?

This doesn't mean that I'm a doormat, though. When people keep breaking their commitments, I notice that I mirror their movement by moving away myself. I don't make a third dinner date with someone who hasn't shown up for the first two. If someone cancels twice, I trust him to do what he does, and making a third date is not efficient. If he invites me a third time, I might say, "I hear that you *want* to show up, I know you did your best, I realize that your mind can't remember when it doesn't remember, and because we're together *now*, let's use this time. I don't want to make a date with you, but let's talk now. I'm totally available. Tell me everything."

When you become a lover of what is, the war is over. Since I don't believe my thoughts, I have no hopes, fears, or expectations; I'm a woman without a future. I live in the open space where everything comes to me. Reality is a very fine place to be. And guess what? Any time you question your mind, you discover that that's where you are, too.

50

She holds nothing back from life;
therefore she is ready for death.

How can anyone describe the indescribable, or bring into existence what is just a mirror image of reality? There are names for it: arm, leg, sun, moon, ground, salt, water, shirt, hair—names that can only reflect the unseeable, the unknowable. There are many names for what can never be named. When you oppose it, when you experience anything as separate or unacceptable, the result is suffering, and inquiry can bring you back to the peace you felt before you believed that thought. It can bring you back to the world prior to any problems. When there is no opposition, the colors no longer clash, music becomes beautiful again, no dance is out of step, and every word is poetry.

Reality is the always-stable, never-disappointing base of experience. When I look at what really is, I can't find a me. As I have no identity, there's no one to resist death. Death is everything that has ever been dreamed, including the dream of myself, so at every moment I die of what has been and am continually born as awareness in the moment, and I die of that, and am born of it again. The thought of death excites me. Everyone loves a good novel and looks forward to how it will end. It's not personal. After the death of the body, what identification will mind take on? The dream is over, I was absolute perfection, I could not have had a better life. And whatever I am is born in this moment as everything good that has ever lived.

I know that there is never anything to lose, so it's easy for me to hold nothing back from life. And because I give it everything I have, my life is complete in every moment. There is never anything undone. There is no moment in my life when I'm not complete.

When I see only what's real, how can any experience be frustrating? Even when I apparently fail, even when I'm apparently defeated, there is a constant appreciation and joy going on inside me. How fascinating to see me baffled by technology, for example. I'm in an apartment in Amsterdam and have been on the road for almost three months, living in hotel rooms. Finally, an apartment, for six whole days in a row! It's near the park, and it has a kitchen and a big living room overlooking a quiet square. And, heaven of heavens, a washing machine! It can't get any better than this. Hmm. With Fuchs' dystrophy, sometimes I can see and sometimes I can't, and it has been a few days now since I could see clearly. And I absolutely cannot read the dial on the washing machine. So I wait, thinking that maybe in a couple of hours my eyes will clear up. Later I notice, excitedly, that I can read the dial well enough to see words. Of course, the words are in Dutch. I call a Dutch friend, and she translates for me. I guess at what bin to put the soap in. Who needs fabric softener anyway? And, by the way, I hope this really is soap, and if it is, I hope it's for washing machines. I was given a detailed lesson in how to run this machine yesterday, so I have an idea of what to do, but I've forgotten some essential instructions. Oh, well. I start the machine, and I'm thrilled. Clean clothes!

Three hours later, I take a peek. The machine is still going through cycles, and I have lost my vision again. Until the clothes spin and the correct cycle completes, the door on the washing machine won't open. So now I'm turning the dial by sound, with my ear close to it, listening to the clicks, like a safecracker. After the cycle ends, the door still doesn't open. I can't see the dial, I can't figure out the machine,

I don't know what more to do, I call Stephen in and *he* doesn't know what to do, there's a load of wet clothes in the washing machine, the door won't open, I'm not sure if it was soap I put in or if it was in the right dispenser or if the wet clothes are even clean. And I notice that I'm feeling calm—tickled actually, always watching mind and the way of it. There's nothing wrong, everything is right. The thought that the machine should work or that the clothes should get clean never even occurs to me. I'm just watching where reality goes next. It's fascinating. Is the goal to wash the clothes? Is the goal to wash the clothes in this machine? You never know. In another hour or two we may be headed for an adventure at the Laundromat up the street.

Then suddenly I remember that the landlord told me there's a little quirk to the washing machine: you have to turn the dial to a certain place to complete the cycle before the door will open. I turn it, the door opens, and finally, after five hours, voilà! the laundry is done.

51

The Tao gives birth to all beings . . .
creating without possessing,
acting without expecting,
guiding without interfering.

Everything is one but not the same. No two fingerprints are the same, no two blades of grass, no two snowflakes, no two pebbles. All of these together make up the way of it, perfect and undivided. Each apparent separateness is a micro-glimpse of the whole, each word spoken, each syllable broken down, each wave of a hand or crossing of the legs, each squeeze of toothpaste onto the bristles of a toothbrush. Each is different, each is necessary. Someone lives, someone dies, someone laughs, someone grieves. For now, that's the way of it, until it's not.

I look up and there you are. You have never existed before. I am meeting you for the first time, and you're my everything. I love that you appear now. Thoughts might say that we've met before, maybe we've had dinner or worked together, but for me you are entirely new. I notice that you're being breathed and nourished, that you're doing well in your happiness or your sorrow, that you're absolutely supported—the ground supports you, the chair supports you, you even have hair. You are the way of it: my internal, my ever-flowing, creative, all-loving self.

If you ask me to do The Work with you, I'm happy to join you there. Inquiry is where I can be understood. I am you in the answers. We meet in the center. It's the only way I can be seen or understood: in the center, the heart.

Whenever you invite me, I'll jump into your dream. I'll follow you through the tunnel, into the darkness, into the darkest pit of suffering. I'll meet you there, I'll take you by the hand, and we'll walk through it together into the light. There's no place I won't enter. I'm everything, everywhere. What I've heard from many people is "Thank you for going to hell and coming back for me." You are my echo, you are every concept I ever believed when I was so confused. Every suffering that's ever been felt—I'm the teacher of that. I go back for what's left of myself. There's total freedom here: all suffering has ended, for now. And since the external turned out to *be* the internal, as long as there is one person suffering, it's my suffering. I don't experience it from here, but there's no separation. "There" *is* here. And I remember the illusion. Love comes back to connect with itself even in its purest state. That's what I refer to as the reentry. Until you're free, I'm not free. I *know* that you're free. And if you tell me you're not, I understand, because I used to believe that, too.

And, really, I have no ideas about whether you should or shouldn't suffer. I respect your path as much as I respect my own. I understand it if you're mesmerized by your story of who you are and you want to hold on to it for now. If you really *don't* want to suffer, I'm there for you. Through inquiry, I'll meet you as deeply as you want to go. Whatever you say, I'll meet it; whatever you ask for, I'll give. I love you, because I'm totally selfish. Loving you is simply self-love.

I don't change, and I see change in you only if you say so. You are my inner life. You're the voice of my self, reporting my health at all times. Sickness or health—it's all fine with me. You're sad, you're not sad; you don't understand, you understand; you're peaceful, you're upset; you're this, you're that. I am each cell reporting itself. And, beyond all change, I know that each cell is always at peace.

As closely as I can describe it in words, I am your heart. I am what you look like inside yourself. I am the sweetest place you come from. I am no one. I am a mirror. I am the face in the mirror.

52

In the beginning was the Tao.
All things issue from it;
all things return to it.

P eople are fascinated with the origin of things. "When did the universe begin?" they ask. "Where do I come from?" The answers to
questions like these are obvious once you get a little clarity. When did
the universe begin? Right now (if at all). A clear mind sees that any
past is just a thought. There's no proof for the validity of any thought
other than another thought, and even *that* thought is gone, and then
the thought "That thought is gone" is itself gone. There is only now,
and even "now" is a thought of the past. Actually, the universe has no
beginning and no end. It's constantly beginning, and it's always over.
Where do I come from? From this very thought. Oops: now I'm gone.

There's nothing mystical about this. If it seems hard to grasp,
that's because it is so simple and clear that a complicated mind can't
see it. What people call "mystical experiences" may be very clear, too,
and a kind of grace for a while, but they amount to nothing in the
end. They're not experiences to invite or to reject; they're just movements of the mind. You can have the most marvelous revelations, you
can be shown all of physical creation, from the beginning of time
to the end of time, how the universe starts with nothing, goes out to
everything, and how, at the point of infinity, it arcs and comes back

to itself; how it is like a circle of numbers, and each number is not just a number but also an energy or a vibration of light and sound and color, all perfectly coordinated, without separation; how every being, every material object, every atom, is also a vibration and a number, from zero to infinity; how fire is a number, and air and water and stars; how it is all itself coming back to itself, with its full understanding, everything—pencil, cloud, galaxy, ant, atom—vibrating as a different number and frequency; how the numbers go all the way out and all the way back and return to zero; how the whole universe of form, from the beginning to the end of time and everything in between, is happening all at once, in fire, water, ice, air, rock, clay, human, animal, silence—and it all adds up to nothing. You can see the origin of the universe and the ultimate meaning of life, everything anyone has ever longed to see, and it will mean nothing, because ultimately everything in the universe is nothing imagined as something, and you exist prior to anything you think you are. Even if you experience all the levels and dimensions within one thought, all the veils and loops of it, not even the deepest knowledge has meaning. Anyone can step into it at any level, and it would be true. There is nothing that isn't true if you believe it, and nothing that is true, believe it or not. You are awareness. It's all-inclusive; it doesn't leave anything out, not from any of the stages. None of the story is left out.

The truth is that everything comes from the I. If there's no thought, there's no world. Without the I to project itself, there is neither origin nor end. And the I just appears: it doesn't come out of anything and it doesn't return to anything. Actually, even "nothing" is born out of the I, because even it is a concept. By thinking that there is nothing, you continue to create something.

The I is the origin of the whole universe. All thought is born out of that first thought, and the I cannot exist without these thoughts. Every story of enlightenment is gone. It's just one more story about the past. If it happened five seconds ago, it might as well have been a million years. The thoughts are what allow the I to believe that it has an identity. When you see that, you see that there's no you to be enlightened. You stop believing in yourself as an identity, and you become equal to everything.

When mind has nothing to identify as, you experience everything in its beauty as yourself. I used to see my hands and fingers as amazing transparent things. I would marvel at the light bouncing off the fingers, inside and throughout the fingers. It was like watching molecules being born, a body being gathered, all of it radiant, and it wasn't only with my fingers, it was with everything.

Everything is just as beautiful now, only I'm not so shocked. I'm used to whatever universe may appear; it's all acceptable. It's always new, but now it's more ordinary; it has taken on a maturity, a settling-in. At the beginning, in 1986, I lived in a state of continuous rapture, so intoxicated with joy that I felt like a walking lightbulb. But there was a sense of separation in that; I could see how it frightened some people, and how others put me on a pedestal. The radiance continued, but eventually its experience was to appear as ordinary. Until it was ordinary and balanced, it wasn't of much value to people. So if someone asks, it will meet them. It's mature enough just to meet them. Nothing special.

People gradually taught me, through their example, how to communicate. Early on, when someone would say, "It's a nice day," I would often feel like giggling. I might see the statement as the funniest joke I had ever heard. "Ha-ha! That's a good one. They think a day is possible." If someone asked what my name was, I might say, "I don't have one." They would ask, "Who are you?" and I'd say, "I don't know." They would say, "Your name is Katie," and I'd say, "No, it's not." They would say, "You're a woman," and I'd say, "That's not my experience." They would ask, "What do you think?" and I would say, "I don't." They wanted to teach me that I was thinking. A couple of women were adamant. They wanted so badly to prove I was actually thinking that for two whole days they tried to convince me. They said, "You have to be thinking if you're talking." And I'd say, "Well,

A THOUSAND NAMES FOR JOY   153

I'm not." "But you *have* to be." They said that I was in denial, that I was just fooling myself. Finally I understood. I said, "Oh, you believe that if thought arises, you did it." I could hear how they believed that I was thinking. But the truth is that I'm not thinking. Thoughts just arise. Though even that isn't true. And if it were, I'm not *doing* the thinking: I'm being thought.

It became more mature, more grounded. It had to understand the world of its old internal self, it had to get used to its own appearance as a personality, it had to get used to its own mirror image, as people's stories gave it identity. It was like holding up a mirror to a young child, and she doesn't show any interest in it, because she doesn't see the image as herself. Then one day you put a new dress on her, and if she understands that it's an image of herself, she is filled with delight, and when she looks into the mirror she sees the whole world and all the galaxies. That is my body. It's my dress and my nakedness. All things appear simultaneously. All of it is me, now.

Every year what I call "the great scam" becomes more unrecognizable. I move from the truth and say, "It's a tree. It's a sky. I'm a Katie"—for love's sake, to meet people where they are. Its language has become ordinary. It doesn't appear as smarter or dumber than other people. It doesn't appear as more or as less. It just watches and waits. The more it chameleons and takes on sameness, the more powerful it becomes, the more trusted it is, and the more profound is the penetration. I will say or do anything that's natural.

It's mature now. When people ask me my name, I'll say, "Katie." I'll say, "It's cool this evening," or "Come look at the clouds, sweetheart," or "Don't the roses smell sweet?" If you tell me it's a tree, I'll agree with you. So you let me into your heart, and then I penetrate. And if you have no interest in the truth, then we can just sit together and have a wonderful time.

53

The great Way is easy,
yet people prefer the side paths.

The great Way is easy. It's what reveals itself right here, right now. "Do the dishes." "Answer the e-mail." "Don't answer the e-mail." It's the great Way because it's the only way. Whatever you do or don't do is your contribution to reality. Nothing could be easier. Nothing else is required; you can't do it wrong.

The side paths are your judgments about what you're doing or not doing. It makes life extremely difficult when you call what you're doing "wrong," "stupid," or "unnecessary"—when you belittle it after it has been done. To compare what you've done to what you should have done, to think that you need to measure up to some external standard, is a difficult path. What is is always the way it's supposed to be right now, and it's always the story of a past. You can argue with the past all you want, and after you've come up with the best, most persuasive, most humane reasons in the world that it should have been different, the past is what it is. Learn from the past, by all means, but if you feel any guilt or shame about it, you are just inflicting violence on yourself, and violence doesn't work. The clear way, the great Way, is to begin now.

You can't change the projected world, but you can change mind, the projector. Just notice when things are out of balance. You don't have to figure it out. There's a built-in signal that will always let you know: it's called stress. Your unquestioned thoughts about life lead you to believe that there's something out of order, and that can never be true. Stress allows you to know when to inquire. Judge your neighbor, write it down, ask four questions, turn it around. In itself, life is effortless. If you think there's a problem, inquire, until you can see how perfect the way of it is.

54

Whoever is planted in the Tao
will not be rooted up.

We do only three things in life: we sit, we stand, and we lie horizontal. That's about it. Everything else is a story. Life is not difficult; it's your *thinking* that makes it difficult. That's where your happiness or misery comes from. There are two ways to sit or stand or lie horizontal: you can do it comfortably, or you can do it with stress. If you don't love where you are, I invite you to question your beliefs.

It takes a lot of courage to go inside yourself and find genuine answers to the four questions of The Work. When you do, you lose all your stories about the world—you lose the whole world as you understood it to be. Once you question what you believe, you begin to see clearly, because the mind is no longer at war with itself. In fact, you become excited about reality, even about the worst that could happen. You open your arms to reality. Just show me a problem that doesn't come from believing an untrue thought.

Whatever happens, I always look for the gift in it. I don't have eyes for anything else. I know that if I lose anything or anyone, I've been spared. If my husband left me, I'd think, *How do I know that I don't need him? He's gone.* If I were to lose my legs, I'd think, *How do I know that I don't need legs? I don't have them.* Of course, freedom doesn't mean that you let unkind things happen—it doesn't mean passivity or masochism. If someone says he's going to cut off your legs, run!

How do you know that you need cancer? You've got it. But to accept cancer is not to lean back and do nothing; that's denial. You consult the best doctors you can afford, and you get the best treatment available. Do you think your body is going to heal most efficiently when you're tense and fearful and fighting cancer as an enemy? Or when you're loving what is and realizing all the ways in which your life is actually better because you have cancer, and from that calm center doing everything you can to heal? There's nothing more life-giving than inner peace.

The only time you suffer is when you believe a thought that argues with reality. You are the cause of your own suffering—but only all of it. There is no suffering in the world; there's only an uninvestigated story that leads you to believe it. There is no suffering in the world that's real. Isn't that amazing!

Both pleasure and pain are projections, and it takes a clear mind to understand that. After inquiry, the experience of pain changes. The joy that was always beneath the surface of pain is primary now, and the pain is underneath it. People who do The Work stop fearing pain. They relax into it. They watch it come and go, and they see that it always comes and goes at the perfect moment.

My eyes hurt this morning. With Fuchs' dystrophy, there are blisters on the inside of the corneas, and sometimes the pain is intense. In addition, my specialist asked me to put a drop of salt solution in, six to eight times a day; this dries the moisture that causes the cloudy vision, but it's also literally salt in the wound—it adds to the pain of the lesions that form and burst and continue to create scar tissue on the cornea. Still, even after a drop, when I look at my granddaughter's face, all I see is a blur. I notice the thought *How beautiful Marley is!* and then it occurs to me that, given the progression of my disease, the time may come when I'll never see her face again. I understand that it's unnecessary; I can't find one place in me where it ultimately matters. I may never see any of my grandchildren as they grow up, I may never see Stephen's face again, or my children's. And as I realize that, I look for sadness, and I can find only joy. An overwhelming sense of gratitude for life wells up in me, for how full life is and how nothing is ever missing, how everything is the way it's supposed to be. I continue to wait and see if I can find a need for something more, and it doesn't appear.

Another day, sitting in the living room, I pour hot tea from a kettle into a cup, and I don't see that the cup is cracked, and the hot tea spills out onto my left hand. Ow! What an adventure! Even as my hand starts to throb, I'm aware that what I'm watching is absolute perfection. How can I believe that my hand is not supposed to be scalded when it is? Why would I move from reality into a fantasy of what my hand should be? When inquiry is alive inside you, thoughts don't pull you away from loving whatever happens, as it happens.

THE WORK IN ACTION

"She shouldn't have left me."

BRUCE: *I am angry at my girlfriend, Sheila, because she abandoned me, shut me out, and left our relationship.*

KATIE: "She abandoned you"—**is that true?**

BRUCE: Yes, it is. I mean, physically, tangibly, yes, she left the relationship, and emotionally she left the relationship.

KATIE: "She abandoned you"—**can you absolutely know that that's true?**

BRUCE: Yes. That's what happened.

KATIE: **How do you react when you believe that thought?**

BRUCE: I get scared, I get angry, I get defensive.

KATIE: And where do you feel that thought in your body? Where does it hit you?

BRUCE: In my chest. My chest gets really tight. My stomach hurts, I feel a little lightheaded, my pulse starts to race. It starts in my chest but seems to take over my whole body from there.

KATIE: Where does your mind travel when you believe the thought "She abandoned me"?

BRUCE: Well, I go in search of all the appropriate film clips to support that.

KATIE: Exactly so. Isn't it an amazing movie! The thought happens, and the mind supports it with pictures—that's how the false world is born. Keep watching, sweetheart.

BRUCE: Well, it's a library. I have a whole library of film clips.

KATIE: And then don't the films begin to show you where you've failed? And you feel all the guilt and shame.

BRUCE: Yes, that seems to be the pattern.

KATIE: And then the mind attacks her, and then it attacks you.

BRUCE: Right. I get resentful. I resent the hell out of her. Sometimes I think that she's a coldhearted, castrating bitch. And sometimes I think that she was right to leave, because I'm a total loser.

KATIE: I would question the thought "I am a total loser," angel. But do that later. Let's continue with "She abandoned me." **Who would you be without that thought?**

BRUCE: I'd be less angry. Maybe I wouldn't be angry at all. Maybe I wouldn't be so sad. I would free up all that mental space for something else. And I would probably be more present. I wouldn't be so stuck in seeing what I did wrong, what *she* did wrong. I wouldn't blame her so much. That's really painful.

KATIE: Yes, the mind wouldn't have to prove what it doesn't really believe. That would be unnecessary.

BRUCE: Yes, I can see that. I would be much happier. But I really *do* believe that she abandoned me. That's what actually happened. What do I do with that?

KATIE: I hear you, sweetheart. Your answer to questions one and two was yes. You really believe it's true that she abandoned you. In her reality, she may not have abandoned you at all, she may simply have moved on with her life. But you are convinced that she abandoned you. That's your story. Now we're just looking at your answers to questions three and four. We're seeing how you react when you believe that thought, and who you would be without it.

BRUCE: Right. I can't find anything good about how I react when I believe that thought. It's a very painful thought.

KATIE: We're seeing that *with* the thought you're angry and resentful, and *without* the thought you don't have all that stress. So it's the thought that is causing your pain, not your girlfriend.

BRUCE: Wow. That never occurred to me.

KATIE: She has nothing to do with your pain. It's all you. It's all your unquestioned thoughts.

BRUCE: My God! That's amazing.

KATIE: "She abandoned me"—**turn it around.**

BRUCE: Umm . . . I abandoned her?

KATIE: Okay. Now give me three ways that you did that. Give me three *genuine* examples of where you abandoned her in your relationship.

BRUCE: I was afraid you were going to ask that. Well, there were times in the relationship where I didn't follow through on issues I said I would follow through on, because I was afraid it would lead to the explosive situations, sort of emotional mania.

KATIE: Yes. And it's interesting to notice when you defend and justify.

BRUCE: Oh. [Pause.] I did do that, didn't I?

KATIE: Yes. You moved away from inquiry and into your story. Defense and justification keep you from answering the questions. The mind is so stuck in its patterns of proving that it's right that it spins you away from the questions. Just notice that, and gently return to inquiry.

BRUCE: Okay.

KATIE: So that's one way. How else did you abandon her? Give me two more ways.

BRUCE: Umm, I wasn't fully present in the relationship.

KATIE: What did that look like?

BRUCE: I would withdraw, I would stalemate, I would close off to her.

KATIE: That's two. Give me one more way.

BRUCE: Well, she actually moved across the country. So we carried on a long-distance relationship for the last two years. And I let her do that. [He rolls his eyes.] I participated in that, because in some way it felt more comfortable to me, there wasn't so much pressure of making a commitment.

KATIE: Good. That's three.

BRUCE: You know, you're so right about justifying. There's a real strong reaction in me to defend and justify myself, even when I try not to. Wow.

KATIE: Isn't it delicious to notice! To begin to fall in love with the mind—it's brilliant in its ability to prove that what isn't actually is. Can you find another turnaround to "She abandoned me"?

BRUCE: *I* abandoned me.

KATIE: How did you do that? What are some examples?

BRUCE: I wasn't being true to myself. I wasn't being vocal about my needs. And that's just another form of abandonment, ironically. So by not being fully present for myself, I left her as well.

KATIE: Can you find another turnaround?

BRUCE: She *didn't* abandon me? But that's not true. She did!

KATIE: Turnarounds are a way of exploring the truth. Sometimes there are turnarounds that you miss, sometimes there are turnarounds that don't work, and I like to sit in those. The Work is meditation. If you sit in this turnaround for a while, you may find that it's actually truer than your original statement.

BRUCE: I always thought there were just three turnarounds: to the self, to the other, and to the opposite. And then I was talking to a friend, and he said, "I did six turnarounds on one statement! I've got them on a computer template, and they're just blowing my mind!" And I don't understand how that actually happens.

KATIE: Within those three basic turnarounds, sometimes there are others. Some of them work and some don't. Your friend probably took it very slow and spent a long time with his statement. He sounds like he was very open to finding his own truths, and they came to him when it was time, and he just waited, and noticed, and he got what he needed. You can't do this Work wrong, sweetheart. That's not possible. No thought comes ahead of its time. Let's look at your next statement.

BRUCE: *I want Sheila to come back, apologize, and promise to never leave me again. I want her to work on her reflectivity, and see how reacting out of fear hurts me and others. I want her to work on her self-esteem and volatility.* [He laughs.]

KATIE: Then it's not Sheila you want to come back! The woman you're describing isn't her.

BRUCE: Yeah, she's the one I want . . . that's the problem.

KATIE: It can't be Sheila. You want someone who sees how reacting out of fear hurts you. You want someone who has worked more on her self-esteem. *That's* who you want back. And that's not her. "I want you to come back so I can just shape you up."

BRUCE [laughing]: Right.

KATIE: "Come back so that you can be the woman of my dreams, because you're not!"

BRUCE: Right.

KATIE: "In fact, you're not even anyone I want to live with, until I work on you and you shape up. Until you make all those changes that you'll really thank me for later."

BRUCE: Right. So what's the problem? [Everyone laughs.]

KATIE: So it's not *her* you want to come back.

BRUCE: Right. It's not who she is. Oh my God.

KATIE: Good one, huh?

BRUCE: This is really a pattern of mine. When I'm in relationships, or work mode, or anything else, I tend to look at things in terms of potential. In terms of what they could be, as opposed to what they are.

KATIE: Well, then you could tell her, "I want you to come back, because I see you as potentially someone I can accept."

BRUCE [laughing with the audience]: Well, *that's* really alluring. Yeah. But I *did* that. I did that.

KATIE: Well, of course you did that. We do that until we don't. That's been your job. I'm just helping you change professions here. We're seeing who we are without these stories. So, sweetheart, "You want her to come back"—**is that true?**

BRUCE: Um . . .

KATIE: Just take a look at it. Because you may say, "I want you" and then when she comes back, you wonder why you don't want her anymore. "You want her to come back"—**is that true?**

BRUCE: With the list of changes or without?

KATIE: She hasn't changed. She's just Sheila. She's not the new, improved woman of your imagination. Do you want her to come back, just as she is?

BRUCE [after a pause]: Not really. I want her back, but I want her to change.

KATIE: Thank you for noticing. [The audience laughs.] When you love the person you live with, just as she is, you're never surprised; you always find it delightful, because that's the person you've invited back. You just work on yourself. Your partner cannot be the cause of your misery, and she doesn't ever have to change. And then all those things you wanted to change about her become the very things you love, once you have questioned your mind. But just know whom you're inviting back, without deluding yourself.

BRUCE: Okay.

KATIE: Knowing that, potentially, she could change. Who knows? People do change.

BRUCE: Do you believe that?

KATIE: No. [Bruce and the audience laugh.] It's not true. Minds change, and bodies follow.

BRUCE: I see that.

KATIE: So "I want her to come back"—**how do you react when you believe that thought** and she moves away?

BRUCE: Oh, it's painful! I feel like I'm living life with one foot in the future and one foot in the past, and I'm straddling the present. I'm just not here.

KATIE: Your life's on hold.

BRUCE: Exactly.

KATIE: **Who would you be without the thought** "I want her back"? Who would you be if you didn't believe that?

BRUCE: I would be a lot more centered. I would be peaceful, I think—more peaceful. I feel like there would be a space to grow some contentment.

KATIE: That tells me you would be more sane about who it is you want back. Let's turn it around. "I want her back"—**turn it around.**

BRUCE: I want *me* back.

KATIE: Yes. Because when you want her back, you're wanting someone back who doesn't exist, and you lose yourself in that. And it's not fair to her, because she can't be your dream woman. She's her.

BRUCE: Yes. But one of the things I noticed that my mind does—this isn't an isolated incident—is when I get into relationships I have these histories that build up with people, and I give that power over to them, and when they leave, all those histories leave with them. And I feel, "Oh my God, who am I? I have to rebuild my identity again?" And it's so tiring.

KATIE: "You have to rebuild your identity again"—**is that true?**

BRUCE: No. No, it's really not.

KATIE: No, because your identity is already there for you; you don't have to rebuild it. It's there. You wake up, and she's not there— that's your identity. "I am the man who wakes up alone."

BRUCE: Right.

KATIE: "I'm the man who eats breakfast by himself."

BRUCE: That would make a great T-shirt. "I am the man who wakes up alone." [The audience laughs.]

KATIE: That could attract a lot of women! [More laughter.] You have a marketing mind, don't you? But you're attached to the dream of who she is. And she plays the role by trying very hard to be who you want her to be.

BRUCE: Oh, yeah. I see that.

KATIE: And she always falls short. If she did all those things for you, and made all those changes, you would see even higher potential for her.

BRUCE: Yes. I actually got a letter from her a year ago and part of that letter really stood out in my mind, there was a lot of anger in it, and she said, "I took all these classes and communication courses, and I did all this stuff you wanted me to do, and you're *still* not satisfied." And I thought, *Wow, you did that all for me!* And all these red flags went off, and I thought, *Uh-oh! What's going on here?*

KATIE: Well, now you know.

BRUCE: Yeah, now I know.

KATIE: It's right there, in black and white. So read it again.

BRUCE: *I want Sheila to come back, apologize, and promise . . .* [Laughing] Well, now these statements just sound absurd! *I want Sheila to apologize and promise to never leave me again. I want her to work on her reflectivity, and see how reacting out of fear hurts me and others. I want her to work on her self-esteem and volatility,* and blah, blah-blah, blah-blah. [The audience laughs.]

KATIE: Okay, so now you can understand why she moved away. [The audience laughs even harder.]

BRUCE: Yes. Why would you want to be with somebody who is constantly trying to improve you?

KATIE: Well, those are your requirements. And she tried.

BRUCE: Right. But they'll change with somebody else, so I'll have new requirements.

KATIE: Who knows? You might not. It could be that you become so awake to yourself that people who don't attract you won't attract you. Can you hear this?

BRUCE: Yes.

KATIE: People who don't attract you won't attract you, because you won't put all of those requirements on them—your story of their potential, how great they will be if only they do this, this, and this. And then when someone attracts you, it's the real thing. You don't have to change her. You don't have to overhaul her.

BRUCE: So how does that work, because in relationship, it's all about exploring, and . . .

KATIE: If you see her for who she really is, not through her potential, you see that she's a woman without the things that you require. You're being attracted to a woman who's just the way she is. And because your mind is clear, it's the real deal. The woman you're attracted to really is her. Not the one you imagine her to be. And that's what The Work's about. Now let's **turn it around.** "I want me . . ."

BRUCE: I want me to come back to myself, I want me to apologize to myself, I want me to promise to never leave me again.

KATIE: Yes, when you have a partner and when you don't have a partner.

BRUCE: Right, right. With or without a partner. I want me to work on my reflectivity, and see how reacting out of fear hurts me. I want to work on my self-esteem and volatility. Well, that's so true. That *is* what I want.

KATIE: You have potential! [The audience applauds, and Bruce laughs.] You might write her a letter and say, "Here are the things I'm working on."

BRUCE: Poor girl!

KATIE: There's another turnaround.

BRUCE: I want me to come back to me . . .

KATIE: . . . to *her*.

BRUCE: To her? Oh my God. I want me to come back to her. Something in that really stings.

KATIE: Uh-huh.

BRUCE: I want me to apologize to her. Apologize to her? No way! [Everyone laughs.]

KATIE: We like it when apologizing is *their* job.

BRUCE: Wow. I can see that my whole defense thing just went off again.

KATIE: But the statement didn't say, "I want me to go back and marry her and love her forever and accept all this stuff."

BRUCE: Apologize for my part in it.

KATIE: Just to go back to her—read it. "I want me to . . ." [Laughing] No wonder it stung!

BRUCE: I'm glad you think this is funny.

KATIE: No wonder it stung: you left *yourself*.

BRUCE: I want me to apologize to her, and promise to never leave her again.

KATIE: It doesn't have to be physical, honey.

BRUCE: Oh.

KATIE: You don't have to leave her again for these things that she's not capable of—these things that you demand of her. This wasn't her list, it was yours.

BRUCE: Right. Got it. I want me to come back to her, apologize to her, and promise to never leave her again.

KATIE: Keep reading.

BRUCE: This is where I get stuck. *I want her to work on her reflectivity.*

KATIE: "I want me to work on my . . ."

BRUCE: I want me to work on my reflectivity.

KATIE: Let her know that. She'd appreciate it. She might think you could use it.

BRUCE: Oh, she'd hang up in my face.

KATIE: That's okay. This is for you, not for her. You could just tell her, "I am working on my reflectivity, and I apologize for thinking you should work on yours. And also for not accepting you when you were interested in things other than my dream, my list of changes for you." Keep reading.

BRUCE: *I want her to work on her reflectivity, and see how reacting out of fear hurts me and others. I want her to work on her self-esteem and volatility.*

KATIE: **Turn it around.**

BRUCE: I want me to work on my reflectivity, and see how reacting out of fear hurts her and others. I want to work on my self-esteem and volatility. I'm sure I can attach a lot of things to those. I could find where all of these are true about me somewhere.

KATIE: Yes. Which turnarounds are you not getting? You said you're sure you could find them all. Is there one you couldn't find?

BRUCE: Um, volatility. I don't feel like I'm very volatile.

KATIE: You didn't become angry at her?

BRUCE: Yes, I would become angry. Even though it might be one on a scale of one to ten, and her anger is a twenty.

KATIE: Well, that one is volatile—for you. Let's move to your next statement.

BRUCE: Okay. *Sheila shouldn't operate out of fear; she should know what she wants and be proactive, she should be patient and tolerant of other people's feelings and processes.* [Everyone laughs.] Oh, God, I'm so embarrassed.

KATIE: Is there anything more exciting than you?

BRUCE: No, this is great. My ego is just melting away up here.

KATIE: Yes, I see that. We'll skip the questions. Just **turn it around.**

BRUCE: *I* shouldn't operate out of fear. *I* should know what I want. Hmm. *I* should be patient and tolerant of other people's feelings and processes.

KATIE: Yes. Especially of Sheila's. That can run very deep. Look at how you treated her when you believed these thoughts. It's like having someone in a lab, where we're always trying to re-create them. And she didn't ask for that. We tell them we love them, and yet they're not good enough, we have to re-create them, and it's very confusing for our partners.

BRUCE: So do you think that because I was in that mode, I didn't love her?

KATIE: Only you can know that, honey. She wasn't the one you wanted, she was the woman you wanted to change. You loved the woman of the future.

BRUCE: Not who she really was. So I was loving a fictionalized version of her.

KATIE: Yes, a potential one. You added qualities to her, and you wanted the potential her. It's like you're God, creating Eve.

BRUCE: Um-hmm.

KATIE: And Adam. You do this with yourself, too.

BRUCE: How so?

KATIE: You try to re-create yourself, too. Look how your mind reacts if you do something that doesn't live up to your expectations. You try to re-create yourself. And if your mind is like a lot of minds, it could be brutal. "How could you do it again? You never get it right. How could you think that, how could you say that? Why did you do that?"

BRUCE: Yes, you're so right. I'm just as hard on myself.

KATIE: As though that violent mode will create something different.

BRUCE: Yes, I have a whole story about that. I'm already some seventy-five-year-old crotchety old man in a bingo parlor. [As a bingo announcer] "G-7." [The audience laughs.]

KATIE: Can you find another turnaround? "Sheila should . . ."

BRUCE: Sheila *should* operate out of fear?

KATIE: Yes.

BRUCE: Okay, so this is just kind of accepting what she really is?

KATIE: Well, let's see.

BRUCE: I'm in a hurry!

KATIE: Well, then look to yourself. See if this is true for you.

BRUCE: Sheila should operate out of fear.

KATIE: Yes, honey.

BRUCE: She should *not* know what she wants.

KATIE: Now you *are* meeting her.

BRUCE [after a pause]: . . . and she shouldn't be patient and tolerant of other people's feelings or their processes.

KATIE: That's Sheila. Isn't she adorable?

BRUCE: That's . . . yeah. So *I* should do this. I should be patient and tolerant.

KATIE: Only if you want to live a happy life. You were like a dictator. You expected *her* to live it. So when you question your mind and get a clue, you get to live it first, and then you teach us our potential.

BRUCE: I see.

KATIE: But you have to live it first—just to make sure that it's possible. Because you may be teaching the impossible. Until you can teach it, learn it. And when you learn it, you *can* teach it—through example, though, not through preaching and scolding and rejecting. Let's look at the next statement.

BRUCE: Okay. What I wrote on my Worksheet was . . . The question is, "What do you want them to do?" And just out of anger I wrote, *I don't want anything from Sheila. I don't need her. She's not in charge of my happiness.* But do you want to know what I really wanted to write?

KATIE: Yes.

BRUCE: *I need Sheila to apologize for her betrayal.*

KATIE: Let's move back to the first statement. **Turn it around,** and be very gentle, and open your heart.

BRUCE: Okay.

KATIE: "I . . ."

BRUCE: I don't need anything from myself.

KATIE: And continue reading.

BRUCE: I am in charge of my happiness.

KATIE: "I am *not* . . ."

BRUCE: I am *not* in charge of my happiness?

KATIE: That's why I asked you to open your mind and your heart. Try it again.

BRUCE: Okay. I don't need anything from myself. I am not in charge of my happiness. [Pause.] This is a little confusing. Is anybody else confused, or just me? [The audience laughs.] You get it? I guess what's confusing me here is that I'm not in charge of my own happiness.

KATIE: Who would you be without your stressful thoughts? All that happiness is already supplied, but the unquestioned mind is so loud, you don't realize the happiness underneath that mind.

BRUCE: Oh, okay, I see . . . okay.

KATIE: You're not in charge of it. It's already there for you. I don't have to do anything for my happiness; I just notice the world without my story, and in that I notice that I'm happy. It's always supplied.

BRUCE: Oh.

KATIE: But the unquestioned mind fights against anything that would bring you joy. My friend Lesley and I were laughing yesterday, because she felt like she was going to throw up, she had a few thoughts about it—they didn't mean much to her—she walked upstairs, she threw up, there was nothing much to throw up, and she just noticed and walked back down. It was over. So reality looks like this: woman throwing up; woman walking back to room.

BRUCE: Another teacher! This is great!

KATIE: Lesley's a wonderful teacher. It was not even an event. She went out, she came back. She has questioned her mind, and what she found under the stressful thoughts was happiness.

BRUCE: Your original nature.

KATIE: Which is always supplied. These turnarounds are meditation. If they don't make sense to you, sit in them. Let's hear the next thing you wrote.

BRUCE: *I need Sheila to apologize for her betrayal.*

KATIE: **Is that true?**

BRUCE: No. That seems ridiculous to me now.

KATIE: **How do you react when you believe the thought** "I need her to apologize," and she doesn't?

BRUCE: I withdraw. I feel isolated and angry.

KATIE: And then where does your mind travel? What other feelings do you have when you believe the thought "I need her to apologize," and the apology doesn't come?

BRUCE: I feel trapped, I feel like I'm waiting for something. I feel resentful, as if she owes me something.

KATIE: Close your eyes and look at the mental pictures that come up when you believe the thought "I need her to apologize." How does your mind attack her?

BRUCE: I see her as very powerful, because she has something that I need, she's in complete control. I also see her as hard-hearted, unkind. I see myself at her feet, clinging to her, cringing, waiting for her to apologize. Hmm, that's kind of cool. Not the feelings, I mean, but it's cool that I can see what I do.

KATIE: Yes, it's very cool. You're getting a little self-realization here. Okay, let's look at the next one.

BRUCE: "What do you think of them?" *Sheila is spontaneous, extroverted, manic, immediate, emotional, dependent, and naïve; she is sensitive, brilliant, and the kindest person I have ever met.*

KATIE: So, look at the list. Read the list again the way you wrote it.

BRUCE: Okay. *Sheila is spontaneous, extroverted, manic, immediate, emotional, dependent, and naïve* . . .

KATIE: ". . . and I want her to come back."

BRUCE [laughing]: ". . . and I want her to come back." Yes. There's a certain charm to it.

KATIE: You know, there is, if you could really hear yourself say that.

BRUCE: Yes. She's lovely. She just . . . I drive myself crazy.

KATIE: Now **turn it around.** "I am . . ."

BRUCE: I am spontaneous, extroverted, manic, immediate, emotional, dependent, and naïve . . .

KATIE: Especially about Sheila.

BRUCE: Yes. It's ironic. I immediately wanted to go back and blame her.

KATIE: Yes, but you immediately noticed that. Isn't that wonderful? You just notice, and begin again—and smile. You noticed, you smiled—that's a good thing.

BRUCE: Yes . . . here I am, doing it again!

KATIE: Wonderful. Let's go to the next one.

BRUCE: *I don't ever want to be abandoned and feel judged intimately again, feel shut out, and be incapacitated by pain.*

KATIE: **Turn it around.**

BRUCE: Yes. This is always the hard one.

KATIE: "I'm willing . . ."

BRUCE: I'm willing . . . ah . . .

KATIE: Yes, I'm willing, if that's the way of it, because it's not as though I had a choice. Thought appears.

BRUCE: I'm willing to be abandoned, and I'm willing to feel judged intimately, and I'm willing to feel shut out, and be incapacitated by pain.

KATIE: Yes, because that could happen. It could happen in life, and if not in life, it could happen in your mind—thoughts are like that. Until we understand them, we believe them. And when we believe them, the stress brings us back into inquiry. The Work wakes us up to what's real and what's imagined. It shows us the difference.

BRUCE: So it's not about painful things not happening. And it's not about those feelings at the time that seemed so real; it's about noticing in the present moment what the reality is.

KATIE: Yes. Exciting, isn't it? Now say the sentence with "I look forward to . . ."

BRUCE: That's a tough one for me. I look forward to being abandoned. I look forward to being judged intimately. I look forward to feeling shut . . . I look forward to feeling shut out and incapacitated by pain.

KATIE: "I look forward to her leaving me again." Whoever it is you imagine you want to live with.

BRUCE: Right. We'll call her "Ms. X."

KATIE: Yes. So look forward to it. It could happen. And you may have heard me say that whenever someone leaves me, I've been spared. There's no exception to that. Look at who left you—you've been spared. The woman of your imagination, who couldn't live up to your standards. And that's the one you longed for to the point where you condemned the real Sheila because she wasn't that one.

BRUCE: Amazing. I really do see that. Thank you, Katie.

KATIE: You're welcome.

55

She lets all things come and go
effortlessly, without desire.

A nyone in harmony with what is has no past to project as a future,
so there's nothing she expects. Whatever appears is always fresh,
brilliant, surprising, obvious, and exactly what she needs. She sees
that it's a gift she has done nothing to deserve. She marvels at the way
of it. She doesn't make a distinction between sound and no sound,
speaking of it or living it, seeing it or being it, touching it or feeling it
touch her. She experiences it as constant lovemaking. Life is her own
love story.

For her, everything is new. She has never seen it before. She has
no belief that would detract from what it really is. In the innocence of
not-knowing, in the wisdom of not needing to know, she can see that
everything as it appears in the moment is always benevolent.

She lets all things come because here they come anyway; it's not
as if she had a choice. She lets all things go because there they go,
with or without her consent. She delights in the coming and the
going. Nothing comes until she needs it, nothing goes until it's no
longer needed. She is very clear about this. Nothing is wasted; there's
never too much or too little.

She doesn't expect results, because she has no future. She realizes the efficiency, the necessity of the way of it, how full it is, how rich, beyond any concept she could have of what it should be. In that realization her life is always renewed. She herself is the way of it, always opening to what comes, always contented.

56

Be like the Tao.
It can't be approached or withdrawn from,
benefited or harmed,
honored or brought into disgrace.

My husband told me about Socrates. Socrates said, "If I'm wise, the only reason is that I know I don't know." I love that! I love that Socrates helped people question their beliefs, and that when the time came for him to drink the hemlock, he did it cheerfully. He wasn't scaring himself or making himself sad, like his dear, unconscious disciples, by projecting a non-existent past onto a non-existent future. He wasn't identifying with a body. When mind leaves the body, we throw it in the ground and walk away. He understood that whatever happens, reality is good. That would bring cheer to anyone's heart. I don't know a thing about his philosophy, but Socrates seems to me like someone who was loving what is.

When your heart is cheerful and at peace, it doesn't matter what you do or don't do, whether you live or die. You can talk or stay silent, and it's all the same. Some people think that silence is more spiritual than speech, that meditation or prayer brings you closer to God than watching television or taking out the garbage. That's the story of separation. Silence is a beautiful thing, but it's no more beautiful than the sound of people talking. I love it when thoughts pass through my mind, and I love it when there are no thoughts. Thoughts can't ever be a problem for me, because I have questioned them and seen that no thought is true.

If you learn to meditate, the mind becomes quiet, you can become very calm, and then it can happen that when you're back in your ordinary life and you get a parking ticket, wham! you're upset. It's easy to be spiritual when things are going your way. When thoughts are simply observed and not investigated, they retain the power to cause stress. You either believe your thoughts or you don't; there's no other choice. They're like someone whispering to you; you aren't really listening, so you don't react. But if you hear that person loud and clear, you can't disregard what he's saying and you may react to it. With inquiry, we don't just notice our thoughts, we see that they don't match reality, we realize exactly what their effects are, we get a glimpse of what we would be if we didn't believe them, and we experience their opposites as being at least equally valid. An open mind is the beginning of freedom.

You can't let go of a stressful thought, because you didn't create it in the first place. A thought just appears. You're not doing it. You can't let go of what you have no control over. Once you've questioned the thought, you don't let go of it, *it* lets go of *you*. It no longer means what you thought it meant. The world changes, because the mind that projected it has changed. Your whole life changes, and you don't even care, because you realize that you already have everything you need.

This goes beyond simple awareness. You meet your thoughts with understanding, which means that you can love them unconditionally. And until you deeply see that not even thoughts exist, you may spend your whole life controlled by them or struggling against them. Just noticing your thoughts works while you're meditating, but it may not work so well when you get the parking ticket or when your partner leaves you. Do you just notice your feelings without a residue? I don't think so. We're not there until we are. When we go inside and truly meet those thoughts with understanding, the thoughts change. They're seen through. And then, if they ever arise again, we just experience clarity—a clarity that includes everyone.

57

Let go of fixed plans and concepts,
and the world will govern itself.

When you follow the simple way of it, you notice that reality holds all the wisdom you'll ever need. You don't need any wisdom of your own. Plans are unnecessary. Reality always shows you what comes next, in a clearer, kinder, more efficient way than you could possibly discover for yourself.

Last week, in Copenhagen, I bought a black eye patch to rest my right eye when it hurts—my pirate costume. My eyes are seeing less, for longer periods of time, and the pain has increased. The cells in my corneas seem to be dying at a very fast rate. I'm excited to find out what blind people know: the kindness of a world without vision, how the other senses become more acute, how the hands learn to feel their way, how ready friends and strangers are to help.

It turns out that I may or may not go blind. Before I left for my summer tour in Europe, a specialist told me that there is such a thing as cornea transplant surgery. Good. One moment there's no cure, and the next moment there is. He said that I wouldn't be a candidate for another four or five years. Good. Stephen does some research and learns that if I'm going to have surgery, the sooner the better. Good. I'll be able to see with new eyes. He does more research, and we learn that the surgery has repercussions: uncomfortable stitches in the eyes, and twelve to eighteen months' recovery time. I hear from a woman who still has six stitches in her eye after sixteen months, 20/500 vision, and a lot of pain. Good: I can do that. People say, "Katie, stop traveling the world." Is that the way of it? Who knows? Success or no success with the surgery, whether my body rejects the new cornea or accepts it, whether I see or not, I have no experience with traveling under such circumstances. Reality will let me know. What it shows me for the present is to keep moving.

Now, through the Internet, Stephen discovers that there's a new kind of cornea transplant surgery ("cutting-edge," he says, with a smile) called DSEK—Descemet's stripping endothelial keratoplasty—and the leading practitioner is Dr. Mark Terry in Portland, Oregon. It's a one-hour procedure, with no stitches, or two or three at most, that transplants just the endothelium (inner layer) of the cornea, and it has a recovery time of weeks or less. Good. Then he finds that the director of one of the Fuchs' online groups has been pleading, "No, no, no, don't do that, it's experimental, there's not enough data, the Fuchs' dystrophy can return if they don't remove the whole cornea, don't let them use you as a guinea pig!" Good: maybe the traditional surgery is the way. He does more research, talks to some doctor friends, asks a lot of questions, and we're back to the new surgery. Good: that will be easier. How do I know to have surgery? I don't need my eyes, after all. But the pain is getting worse, and at times it is exhausting; it lessens my efficiency in sharing inquiry with people. That shows me the way of it. And right here, right now, nothing has happened, and I can't know what will happen.

I am dictating this after putting drops of eye-pain medication in my right eye. I've been doing my job, a weekend intensive, and then I signed books for an hour or so until my eye stung. What a beautiful moment: Stephen typing my words, the breeze flowing through the open terrace door of the hotel room, the Stockholm sky, the gratitude I'm feeling for two doctors—Pascale's mother, who express-mailed me emergency eyedrops from France, and Gustav's father, who prescribed another brand here in Stockholm. They, too, are the way of it, allowing me to continue to function in this moment. Tomorrow morning, Gustav will pick us up after breakfast and drive us to the airport for our flight to Amsterdam. Who knows how my eye condition will turn out? I only know that it's a good thing, as I sit here, doing what I do, being what it is.

Whose corneas will show up? Who will die and give me new vision, if the surgery works? Like me, like you, he or she will die perfectly on time, not a moment too early or too late, and I will inherit the corneas living in that person now—a woman, a man? Old, young? Black, white, yellow? (One dear man in Germany, who loves The Work, offered to donate his corneas. Stephen thanked him and said that he didn't qualify, since he wasn't dead.) I love the way of it. I love that when I die, my body parts, too, will be recycled. Take my heart, my organs, my secondhand eyes; take whatever you need, whatever is usable—they don't belong to me anyway, and they never have.

I look forward to being blind if the surgery doesn't work. I've already been there, almost. I have walked through airport terminals unable to see the signs or read the monitors, I have walked through hotels when the world was a total blur, I have stood in front of a thousand people when I was unable to see raised hands, in a world without faces, without colors—a beautiful world, and very simple to live in. Stephen can see and read without glasses, and at the hotel breakfast buffet I am quick to be on my own as he points out where the soft-boiled eggs are, where the decaf is, where the bread goes into the toaster, where the yogurt and fruit are. I know that I don't need to know anything, and perception shows me shadows, textures, the feel and glow of the world. I gather my food and walk across the large dining room with him, looking for the man who is to join us for the breakfast business meeting. As I walk, everything is dark, and yet there are differences, shadows dark and darker. A shadow moves. I say, "Is that Peter, sweetheart?" And Stephen answers, "Yes. There he is." Without him, I would have had no difficulty walking up and saying,

"Peter, is that you?" And today, the way of it is so kind that there are no obstacles, no chairs out of order, no objects on the floor to trip over.

I always know that the way is clear. And when I trip over an obstacle, I enjoy myself all the way to the ground. Falling is equal to not falling. Getting up again and not being able to are equal. The only way you can know the way of it is to join it without separation. It's constant lovemaking, with no other lover than what is.

I see the common good everywhere. The common good looks like entire villages being wiped out by one tsunami. It looks like one man losing his legs, another man getting the raise that he worked so hard for, a woman so obese that she can't bend over. It looks like the stench coming from the sewer, or the clouds as they slowly move across the blue sky. I no longer believe that the man with no legs shouldn't have lost his legs. I see that he wants them, I see that he thinks he needs them, and I see the heartbreak that comes from believing that. I see that his war with reality is causing all his misery. Misery can never be caused by loss of legs; it can only arise from his desire for what's not.

"I should," "I shouldn't," "you should," "you shouldn't," "I want," "I need"—these unquestioned thoughts distort the appearance of the good that is as common as grass. When you believe them, you make your mind small, and small-mindedness doesn't allow you to see why the loss of legs is good, why blindness is good, sickness, hunger, death, a village wiped out, the whole apparent world of suffering. You stay unaware of the good that is all around you, you block out the elation you'd feel when you finally recognized it. Whatever you think, reality is the natural way of it. It won't bend to your ideas of what it should be, and it won't wait for your consent. It will remain just as it is, pure goodness, whether or not you understand.

58

Try to make people moral,
and you lay the groundwork for vice.

Being present means living without control and always having your needs met. For people who are tired of the pain, nothing could be worse than trying to control what can't be controlled. If you want real control, drop the illusion of control. Let life live you. It does anyway. You're just telling the story about how it doesn't, and that's a story that can never be real. You didn't make the rain or the sun or the moon. You have no control over your lungs or your heart or your vision or your breath. One minute you're fine and healthy, the next minute you're not. When you try to be safe, you live your life being very, very careful, and you may wind up having no life at all. Everything is nourishment. I like to say, "Don't be careful; you could hurt yourself."

You can't make people moral. People are what they are, and they'll do what they do, with or without our laws. Remember the Prohibition amendment? I hear that it was passed by well-intentioned, moral people, who just wanted to save the rest of us from the temptation of alcohol. Of course it failed, because sobriety can come only from the inside. You can't force people to be sober or honest or kind. You can say "Thou shalt not" till you're blue in the face, and they'll do it anyway.

The best way, the *only* effective way, is to serve as an example and not to impose your will. I used to try to make my children moral by telling them what they should do, what they shouldn't do, what they should like, what they shouldn't like. In my confusion, I was trying to be a good mother, and I thought that this was the way to make them good people. When they didn't do what I wanted, I would shame or punish them, believing that it was for their own good. So in reality what I taught them was to break my laws and be very careful not to get caught. I taught them that the way to have peace in our home was to sneak and lie. Many of the things I was teaching them not to do I had done myself and hadn't admitted to them, and some of the things I was still doing even as they watched. I expected them not to do these things simply because I said so. It didn't work. It was a recipe for confusion.

I lost my children twenty years ago. I came to see that they were never mine to begin with. That was an extreme loss: they truly died to me. I discovered that who I thought they were had never existed at all. And my experience of them now is more intimate than I can describe. Today, when my children ask me what they should do, I say, "I don't know, honey." Or, "Here's what I did in a similar situation, and it worked for me. And you can always know that I'm here to listen and that I'm always going to love you, whatever decision you make. You'll know what to do. And also, sweetheart, you can't do it wrong. I promise you that." I finally learned to tell my children the truth.

It's painful to think you know what's best for your children. It's hopeless. When you think that you need to protect them, you're teaching anxiety and dependence. But when you question your mind and learn how not to be mentally in your children's business, finally there's an example in the house: someone who knows how to live a happy life. They notice that you have your act together and that you're happy, so they start to follow. You have taught them everything they know about anxiety and dependence, and now they begin to learn something else, something about what freedom looks like.

That's what happened with my children. They just don't see a lot of problems anymore, because in the presence of someone who doesn't have a problem, they can't hold on to one. If your happiness depends on your children being happy, that makes them your hostages. I think I'll just skip them, and be happy from here. That's a lot saner. It's called unconditional love.

Why would I give my children advice when I can't possibly know what's best for them? If what they do brings them happiness, that's what I want; if it brings them unhappiness, that's what I want, because they learn from that what I could never teach them. I celebrate the way of it, and they trust that, and I trust it.

59

She has no destination in view
and makes use of anything
life happens to bring her way.

When you have no destination in view, you can go anywhere. You realize that whatever life brings you is good, so you look forward to it all. There's no such thing as adversity. Adversity is just an unquestioned thought.

Without a belief, there's no separation. Adversity and good fortune are equal. You can wake up on Mars, you can find yourself in hell, and there's no problem, because The Work is alive inside you. You can flip into the most unusual mind-states, into emotions that you've been hiding from yourself for decades. You can enter the worst of your fears, and with inquiry, it doesn't matter where you go or how you appear. Without a belief, you are all things. And if you get stuck in a particular identity, you have inquiry to unstick you.

One day in 1986, as I was walking in a shopping mall, I saw a very old woman coming toward me on a walker. She looked like she was in her nineties. Her back was bent, and her face grimaced from what appeared to be pain. As I continued to walk, I noticed, to my horror, that I was looking out through this old woman's eyes at the woman I had been, the one with Katie's body, so healthy, agile, and as bright as all the lights in the world. As I watched her, the bright one began to round the corner in her usual fast-paced, carefree manner, and I realized that I was now the old woman. I felt her pain—it wasn't hers now but mine. I smelled my putrid odor. I became aware of my body's flesh disconnected and hanging from its bones. The flesh was wrinkled and gray, with no muscles to hold it. The pain shot through my joints with each movement. The slowness of my motion was infuriating. The thought that accompanied the anger was "I want to move as fast as that young woman. It's not fair."

And then the full horror of the situation appeared. If I were to give it words, the thought would be "Oh, my God, I'm trapped here! I'm supposed to be the young, bright one! There's been a mistake, I'll never get out, I'll be like this forever!" Immediately inquiry arose: "I am this"—is it true? Is it true that I am this forever? How do I react when I believe that? What would I be without the thought? The questioning, too, was beyond words. It didn't come after the wordless thought: thought and questions arose at the same instant and canceled each other out. The horror was equivalent to a deep gentleness, a caressing, a full, immovable acceptance. There was no discomfort. It began, from its new position, to celebrate the whole life of itself, to love itself as the old woman, and to appreciate the slow pace, the withered flesh, the pain, the stench. The stench was as sweet as the fragrance of spring. I was able to love that it had found the perfect home for a me. There was no longer even the slightest desire to be anywhere else. I wanted nothing other than what is. And as soon as I realized this, I found myself, to my amazement, rounding the corner of the mall as the body of the fast-paced, bright woman who had apparently been lost to me forever.

I had come to feel just as comfortable in that decaying old body as I am here, but now it was a Katie. And people wonder why I can look at my hand and become ecstatic. It's no different from being trapped forever in a body that was almost dead. Inquiry can hold any condition, whatever it is, in a state of loving awareness. After that experience, everything was child's play, the freedom of being everywhere, the dance and the bodilessness of it all.

Inquiry is grace. It wakes up inside you, and it's alive, and there's no suffering that can stand against it. It will take you over, and then it doesn't matter what life brings you, "good" or "bad." You open your arms to the worst that can happen, because inquiry will continue to hold you, safely, sweetly, through it all. Even the most radical problem becomes just a sweet, natural happening, an opportunity for your own self-realization. And when others are experiencing terror, you are the embodiment of clarity and compassion. You are the living example.

60

*Give evil nothing to oppose
and it will disappear by itself.*

Life is simple. Everything happens *for* you, not *to* you. Everything happens at exactly the right moment, neither too soon nor too late. You don't have to like it—it's just easier if you do. If you have a problem, it can only be because of your unquestioned thinking. How do you react when you believe that the past should have been different? You scare yourself stuck, because what you resist persists. You get to keep your stressful world, a world that doesn't exist except in your imagination; you get to stay in the nightmare. It hurts to oppose reality, because in opposing reality, you are opposing your very self.

When you know how to question your thoughts, there's no resistance. You look forward to your worst nightmare, because it turns out to be nothing but an illusion, and the four questions of The Work provide you with the technology to go inside and realize that. You don't have to grope in the dark to find your way to freedom. You can just sit down and give it to yourself, anytime you want.

Nineteen years ago a doctor removed a large tumor from my face. I had found inquiry—inquiry had found me—so I didn't have a problem with the tumor. On the contrary: I was happy to see it come, and I was happy to see it go. It was actually quite a sight, and before it was removed I loved being out there in public. People would look at it and pretend not to be looking, and that tickled me. Maybe a little girl would stare at it, then her parents would whisper to her and yank her away. Did they think they would hurt my feelings, or that I was some sort of freak? I didn't feel like one. That tumor on my face was normal for me; it was reality. Sometimes I would catch someone looking at it, then he would look away, then after a while he would look again, then look away, look again, look away. And finally our eyes would meet, and we would both laugh. Because I saw the tumor without a story, eventually he could see it that way, too, and it was just funny.

Everything turns out to be a gift—that's the point. Everything that you saw as a handicap turns out to be the extreme opposite. But you can only know this by staying in your integrity, by going inside and finding out what your own truth is—not the world's truth. And then it is all revealed to you. There isn't anything you have to do. The only thing you're responsible for is your own truth in the moment, and inquiry brings you to that.

I once did The Work with a woman who was ashamed of her fingers. She had developed rheumatoid arthritis when she was seventeen, and she believed that her fingers were deformed. They weren't normal, she thought, and she suffered a lot from that belief; she was embarrassed even to let people see them. But her fingers *were* normal: they were normal for *her*. They were the fingers she had woken up with every morning since she was seventeen. For twenty-seven years they were her normal fingers. She just hadn't noticed.

How do you react when you believe that what is isn't normal for you? Shame, sadness, despair. Who would you be without that thought? At ease with your condition and loving it, whatever it is, because you would realize that it is completely normal, for you. Even if 99 percent of other people look a different way, their normal isn't your normal: *this* is your normal. That dear woman's argument with reality was what caused her suffering, not her fingers.

Give us permission, through you, to have a flaw, because flaws are the norm. When you hide your flaws, you teach us to hide ours. I love to say that we are just waiting for one teacher, just one, to give us permission to be who we are now. You appear as this, big or small, straight or bent. That's such a gift to give. The pain is in withholding it. Who else is going to give us permission to be free, if not you? Do it for your own sake, and we'll follow. We're a reflection of your thinking, and when you free yourself, we all become free.

61

Humility means trusting the Tao.

No one has ever known the answer to *Why?* The only true answer is *Because*. Why do the stars shine? Because they do. Why is the glass sitting on the table? Because it is. That's it. In reality there *is* no why. It's hopeless to ask; the question can't go anywhere—haven't you noticed? Science may give you an answer, but behind that *because* there's always another *why*. There is no ultimate answer to anything. There's nothing to know, and no one who wants to know. Just have fun with the asking, because there are trillions of answers, as many as the stars in the sky, and not one of them is true. Enjoy the stars, but don't think that there's anything behind them. And, ultimately, do you even care about an answer?

The Work is wonderful, because it leaves you with the real thing, beyond all answers. It leaves you with no concept of who you should be. There are no models, no ideals; the goal isn't to be wise or spiritual. You just notice what is. I like to say, "Don't pretend yourself beyond your own evolution." What I mean by that is "Don't be spiritual; be honest instead." It's painful to pretend that you're more evolved than you are, to be in the position of a teacher when it's kinder to yourself to be in the position of a student. Inquiry is about the truth, which doesn't necessarily look the way you think it's supposed to look. Truth is no respecter of spirituality. It only respects itself, just as it appears now. And it's not serious; it's just God laughing at the cosmic joke.

If someone comes toward you with a gun and says he's going to kill you and you're scared, go ahead and run. That's no less spiritual than any other reaction. But if you don't have a belief about it, you're free. You can run or stay—it doesn't matter, because whatever you do, you're at peace. *Oh,* you might think, *he thinks he's going to kill me.* You could just as well be filing your nails. That's freedom.

62

Why did the ancient Masters esteem the Tao?
Because, being one with the Tao,
when you seek, you find;
and when you make a mistake, you are forgiven.

I love that what is of true value can't be seen or heard. It's nothing and it's everything, it's nowhere and it's right under your nose—it *is* your nose, as a matter of fact, along with everything else. It can't be reached or achieved, because as soon as you start looking for it, you leave it. It doesn't have to be achieved, only noticed.

Nothing anyone says is true, and no thought that arises within you is true. There's nothing. And yet, here is the world again. The sun in the sky. The sidewalk. The dog trotting along on a leash.

When you understand that you're one with reality, you don't seek, because you realize that what you have is what you want. Everything makes sense because you don't superimpose your thinking onto reality. And when you make a mistake, you realize immediately that it wasn't a mistake; it was what should have happened, because it happened. Before the fact, there were infinite possibilities; after the fact, there was only one. The more clearly you realize that *would have, could have, should have* are just unquestioned thoughts, the more you can appreciate the value of that apparent mistake and what it produced. Seeing this is forgiveness in its totality. In the clarity of understanding, forgiveness is unnecessary.

63

Act without doing.

When I pick up one of my adorable little granddaughters, wipe her nose, kiss her, put her in the high chair and feed her, I do this not only for me, but *to* me as well. Loving her is loving myself. I don't see any difference. And because I love myself, I can love everyone who comes into my life. At the age of forty-three, I became my first child. I loved me, and that love was without condition. It's the power of one. Because I loved me—this one apparent person—hundreds of thousands of people are learning to love themselves. That's what they tell me.

I fell in love with myself one morning in February of 1986. I had checked myself into a halfway house in Los Angeles after years of suicidal depression. A week or so later, as I lay on the floor of my attic room (I felt too unworthy to sleep in a bed), a cockroach crawled over my foot, and I opened my eyes. For the first time in my life, I was seeing without concepts, without thoughts or an internal story. All my rage, all the thoughts that had been troubling me, my whole world, *the* whole world, was gone. There was no me. It was as if something else had woken up. *It* opened its eyes. *It* was looking through Katie's eyes. And it was crisp, it was bright, it was new, it had never been here before. Everything was unrecognizable. And it was so delighted! Laughter welled up from the depths and just poured out. It breathed

197

and was ecstasy. It was intoxicated with joy: totally greedy for everything. There was nothing separate, nothing unacceptable to it. Everything was its very own self. For the first time I—it—experienced the love of its own life. I—it—was *amazed*!

All this took place beyond time. But when I put it into language, I have to backtrack and fill in. While I was lying on the floor, I understood that when I was asleep, prior to cockroach or foot, prior to any thoughts, prior to any world, there is nothing. In that instant, the four questions of The Work were born. I understood that no thought is true. The whole of inquiry was already present in that understanding. It was like closing a gate and hearing it click shut. It wasn't I who woke up: inquiry woke up. The two polarities, the left and right of things, the something/nothing of it all, woke up. Both sides were equal. I understood this in that first instant of no-time.

To say it again: As I was lying there in the awareness, *as* the awareness, the thought arose: "It's a foot." And immediately I saw that it wasn't true, and that was the delight of it. I saw that it was all backward. It's not a foot; it's not a cockroach. It wasn't true, and yet there was a foot, there was a cockroach. But there was no name for any of these things. There were no separate words for wall or ceiling or face or cockroach or foot or any of it. So it was looking at its entire body, looking at itself, with no name. Nothing was separate from it, nothing was outside it, it was all pulsing with life and delight, and it was all one unbroken experience. To separate that wholeness, to see anything as outside itself, wasn't true. The foot was there, yet it wasn't a separate thing, and to call it a foot, or an anything, felt absurd. And the laughter kept pouring out of me. I saw that *cockroach* and *foot* are names for joy, that there are a thousand names for joy, and yet there is no name for what appears as real now. This was the birth of awareness: thought reflecting back as itself, seeing itself as everything, surrounded by the vast ocean of its own laughter.

Then it stood up, and *that* was amazing. There was no thinking, no plan. It just stood up and walked to the bathroom. It walked straight to the mirror, and it locked onto the eyes of its own reflection, and it understood. And that was even deeper than the delight it had known before, when it first opened its eyes. It fell in love with that being in the mirror. It was as if the woman and the awareness of the woman had permanently merged. There were only the eyes, and a sense of absolute vastness, with no knowledge in it. It was as if I—she—had been shot through with electricity. It was like God giving itself life through the body of the woman—God so loving and bright, so vast—and yet she knew that it was herself. It made such a deep connection with her eyes. There was no meaning to it, just a nameless recognition that consumed her.

Love is the best word I can find for it. It had been split apart, and now it was joined. There was *it* moving, and then *it* in the mirror, and then it joined as quickly as it had separated—it was all eyes. The eyes in the mirror were the eyes of it. And it gave itself back, as it met again. And that gave it its identity, which I call love. As *it* looked in the mirror, the eyes—the depth of them—were all that was real, all that existed. Prior to that, nothing—no eyes, no anything; even standing there, there was nothing. And then the eyes come out to give *it* what it is. People name things a wall, a ceiling, a foot, a hand. But it had no name for these things, because it's indivisible. And it's invisible. Until the eyes. Until the eyes. I remember tears of gratitude pouring down the cheeks as *it* looked at its own reflection. *It* stood there staring for I don't know how long.

These were the first moments after I was born as it, or it as me. There was nothing left of Katie. There was literally not even a shred of memory of her—no past, no future, not even a present. And in that openness, such joy. *There's nothing sweeter than this,* I felt; *there is nothing but this. If you loved yourself more than anything you could imagine, you would give yourself this. A face. A hand. Breath. But that's not enough. A wall. A ceiling. A window. A bed. Lightbulbs. Ooh! And this too! And this too! And this too!* I felt that if my joy were told, it would blow the roof off the halfway house—off the whole planet. I still feel that way.

64

Prevent trouble before it arises.
Put things in order before they exist.

There's no need to put the world in order. Things are already in order, even before they exist. I walk out onto the street, there are people and cars and dogs and birds and plants and litter, and in this marvelous chaos there is a beauty that always delights me. It's all for me, it presents itself to me at the perfect moment, exactly as needed. Though walking down the street doesn't seem like a lot to some people, to me it's a whole world, it's my secret world, where I'm always serving everyone and everything, as they serve me. There's never a task too great or too small, because the only task to accomplish is the one in front of me. It might appear that there are a thousand things to do, but in fact there is never more than one.

I live in constant meditation, and if a thought should ever show up as anything less than goodness, I know that it would spill over to other people as confusion, and those other people are me. My job is to enlighten myself to that, and to love the spent rose, the sound of the traffic, the litter on the ground, and the litterer who gives me my world. I pick up the litter, do the dishes, sweep the floor, wipe the baby's nose, and question anything that would cost me the awareness of my true nature. There's nothing kinder than nothing.

I come home from my walk, make lunch, and as we're eating,

Stephen says, "Look, there are ants in the salad." I continue to chew, and I marvel at the balance of life. I never get more or less protein than I need. Before a rain, the ants move into our kitchen. There is a steady trail of them across the stove and the countertop, and my vision was too foggy to see those marvelous little explorers. Later, sitting on the living room couch, I feel ants on my legs, my arms, in my hair, one by one, little massage therapists, walking over my pressure points, tickling me, sometimes biting me, but only where needed. And I notice my hand moving toward my arm, squeezing an ant between my fingers and killing it as quickly as I would want to die myself. It is my own death I am experiencing, and I love death as I love life. My hand moves to my leg and squeezes two little fellows who are traveling up my calf. I notice the thought "Oh, I'm killing the ants," and I smile. How very strange. The hand keeps moving on its own, without a plan, doing its job. "I" stop it, and I notice later, when I'm not conscious of my murdering ways, that the hand is at it again. When I'm not looking, who is killing the ants? Should I take credit? The hand stops. And who knows what it will be up to next?

My daughter happens to be visiting, and as she leaves the house to buy rice milk for Marley, I tell her, "And, by the way, sweetheart, please buy some ant hotels." Why did I say such a thing? Because I did. That's the way of it. The idea with ant hotels is that the ants are drawn to the poison inside and go back to their nest after eating it and infect the others, and that, supposedly, is the end of the ants in the house. I wonder why killing ants doesn't bother me. And I come to see that my death also is by poison, the things I have done to pollute the water that not only I but everyone drinks, the emissions from my car that poison the very air we breathe. I am so like the ants. And the greed for food that for so many years created guilt in me, as if mind were body and suffering were possible in reality. And the chemicals from the processed food products that I occasionally eat, the many ways that I still poison myself, bring a smile to my face. It's not that I'm masochistic, I love my life, but this continual poisoning is beyond me; it is simply the way of it. Am I breathing? That's how it seems. I live with the ants the way I live with my own dear self. Bodies come and go. And when mind understands itself, when it stops poisoning itself with what it believes to be true, there is no physical experience that it can suffer over.

Two days later, as I sit in my favorite corner of the couch, again I begin to feel little scrambling movements on my hand and my neck. Ants again. It turns out that I am their nest, I am the one they have come back to infect, and I have only bought poison for myself. What goes around comes around. I appreciate that.

65

When they think that they know the answers,
people are difficult to guide.
When they know that they don't know,
people can find their own way.

I don't try to educate people. Why would I do such a thing? My only job is to point you back to yourself. When you discover—inside yourself, behind everything you're thinking—the marvelous don't-know mind, you're home free. The don't-know mind is the mind that is totally open to anything life brings you. When you find it, you have found your way.

I work with four- and five-year-old children who suffer from believing the same concepts that adults believe. These concepts are sacred religions; we're completely devoted to them. "People should come," "People should go," "People should understand me," "I'm too this," "You're too that," "My wife shouldn't lie," "My children should appreciate me," "My husband doesn't love me," "My mother would be much happier if she saw things the way I do." Whatever story we're attached to, that's where our devotion is. There's no room for God in it.

I once worked with a woman in Jerusalem. Her religion was "I should have thin thighs"; she thought that's what would give her what she wanted in life. She was the cutest! And she just wasn't willing to do The Work; she couldn't go inside for an honest answer, because she was terrified that if she answered honestly, she'd end up with fat thighs. She thought she needed fear as a motivation to exercise and eat right. It was obvious that she preferred thin thighs to freedom. She wouldn't take the risk of letting go of control and going deep into herself to see what her own truth was. For her, the sacred concept was thin thighs; for someone else it's more money, for others it's a relationship. I love being with these people. They say they want freedom more than anything in the world, and they cry and beg for help. And as soon as I get anywhere near their sacred concept, these spiritual seekers, who have been on the path for thirty or forty years, have no interest in freedom. Zero. Their true religion has been threatened, and they rush to the ramparts to defend it. I asked her, "Can you absolutely know that it's true that right now your thighs should be thinner than they are?" And you'd be amazed at how fast this woman dodged away. She didn't stop to really ask herself the question, not for an instant. "Yes, I can!" she said. Slam! The gate shuts, the drawbridge goes up, the I-know mind retreats behind its castle walls, ready to defend itself against the whole world. That's why I love to ask someone who sits with me, "Do you really want to know the truth?"

The education you need is within you. How can what is already within you be taught? It can only be realized. If you're willing to go inside and wait for the truth, your inborn wisdom meets the question, and the answer rings true as if it were a tuning fork inside your own being.

When you believe that there is a problem, the Master doesn't try to convince you that there isn't. She is rooted in the place of understanding. She is you reflected back to yourself. She understands that problems are not possible, except when you believe what you're thinking. Only mind lives, if anything lives. The Master will always point you back to your own mind, your own realization. And a part of the deliciousness is to fully meet every suicidal tendency until, in the presence of the Master within you, the self is finally seen for what it isn't.

So the confused mind comes to unlearn its troubling thought through inquiry. It comes not only to see that the thought isn't true, but also to understand the specific effects of believing it, the price in anger or sorrow or resentment that it pays when it believes the thought, and the freedom that would be available without it, and it sees also that the thought's opposites could be at least as true. Eventually it realizes that reality is all mind and that the world changes as its perception changes. To meet the Master with a fearless, open mind is to lose the entire world as you understood it to be. It is to unlearn a cruel world, a world of ravagement, a world where the heart's desire is never attained.

When people think that they know the answers, it's difficult for the Master to help them find their way, because she is dealing with closed minds, and a closed mind is a closed heart. Since she understands that openness never can be forced, she becomes very comfortable and listens, she waits for an opening, the slightest crack, and that is when she penetrates. That is the moment of meeting, of indisputable connection. The other person can close the door, but it's too late, the Master has already entered. And in that instant of entering, everything is changed. Enough clarity gets in to be recognized, and the mind can never be the same again, because like has met like. The two have become one.

Once the Master moves in through that even slightly open door, the student's mind continues to expand, and the natural way to himself appears. It may seem as if he can revert to his former world, but that's not possible. When the mind has seen that it doesn't know what it was so sure of, it begins to unravel, the knots relax and begin to untie themselves. This leaves no job for the Master. It leaves her as no one again.

THE WORK IN ACTION

"My mother should have been allowed to die."

BARBARA: I wrote about my mother, Katie. She died ten days ago. Last year she gave my sister, Laurie, power of attorney over her health decisions. And then she got very sick, and a week before she died, she was in so much pain that she asked to be taken off life support. Laurie lives in a different city, and it took her a week of talking to the doctors and thinking about it before she could make the final decision to pull the plug. I was in the hospital at my mother's bedside, and Laurie wasn't even around. Katie, my mother should have been allowed to die when she wanted to, and I felt so powerless, and so terribly angry at my sister.

KATIE: Okay, sweetheart. Let's hear what you've written.

BARBARA: *I'm angry at my sister for making my mom wait to die.*

KATIE: So you think the best thing for your mother would have been to die a week before she did. "Your sister should have given her approval. She shouldn't have waited a week"—**is that true?**

BARBARA: Yes, it's true. I felt so completely helpless. I had no way to control the situation, and I *knew* that the best thing for her would have been to die, and I had to wait for my sister to decide, and it drove me crazy. I was so desperate. I would have given anything to be able to pull the plug and give my mother what she wanted.

KATIE: Good, sweetheart. I hear that. Now let's go back to inquiry. "Your sister shouldn't have waited"—**can you absolutely know that that's true?**

BARBARA: Well, I . . . It appeared that my mom was suffering a lot during that week that she had to wait . . . And it's *her* body. It's her life, and her decision.

KATIE: Exactly so. And can you know that this week's wait was not the best thing for all three of you? Can you absolutely know that it would have been better the other way?

BARBARA [after a long pause]: No, I can't absolutely know it.

KATIE: That's amazing. Where did that no come from?

BARBARA: Well, I just stopped and listened to your question. It was really hard. I have so many thoughts that make me right and my sister wrong. But when I just listened to the question, it was obvious that I can't *absolutely* know what's best for my mother. However strongly I think I'm right, I just can't know.

KATIE: Yes, honey. There's no mistake. **How do you react when you believe this thought,** "She shouldn't have waited"?

BARBARA: Well, I blame myself, because I think I should have been stronger.

KATIE: Yes. And how does it feel to blame yourself for your mother's pain?

BARBARA: It feels awful. I feel like I didn't come through for her. I feel guilty and weak. And I feel just furious at my sister. I want to wring her neck. I blame her at least as much as I blame myself.

KATIE: Can you see a reason to drop this thought? And I'm not asking you to drop it. You can't let go of a thought, you can only meet it with understanding, and then *it* lets go of *you*.

BARBARA: Well, the thought isn't doing any good now. She's dead.

KATIE: I'm more interested in you. This is about *your* peace. Give me a peaceful reason to keep this thought.

BARBARA: I don't think there is one. It's just making me miserable.

KATIE: **Who would you be without the thought?** Who would you be if you didn't believe that she shouldn't have waited?

BARBARA: I'd be in a relationship with my sister. I'd still be talking to her.

KATIE: Yes, sweetheart. And not waiting, in pain—like your mother.

BARBARA [with tears in her eyes]: Yes, that's true.

KATIE: It's interesting how we try to save them, and we leave ourselves out of it. Now **turn it around.**

BARBARA: She *should* have waited? But my mother was in such pain!

KATIE: Notice when you move from inquiry back into your story, back into defense and justification. "She shouldn't have waited" turned around is "She should have waited." Just sit with that for a while.

BARBARA [after a long pause]: Well, I have to say, the truth is that I can't know whether she should have waited.

KATIE: Good, sweetheart. Now give me three genuine ways that it could be true that she should have waited.

BARBARA: Well, maybe she should have waited so that she could get the best medical advice. [Pause.] And she should have waited till she was certain that the plug should be pulled. [Pause.] And she should have waited so that the whole family could be there when my mother died.

KATIE: Fascinating, isn't it? And there are other ways too, sweetheart. Don't settle for just scratching the surface of things. Everything happens as it should; that's just the way of it. Let's look at your next statement.

BARBARA: *Laurie should listen to others and not do what she thinks is the only way.*

KATIE: **Is that true?**

BARBARA: Well, it's not true, because that's what she does . . .

KATIE: Exactly. It's absolutely not true. How do I know she shouldn't listen to others? She doesn't. That's reality.

BARBARA: I hate that, though.

KATIE: I know! [The audience laughs uproariously.] It's hard not being God. It's hard to be the dictator, when God doesn't listen. **How do you react when you believe that thought?**

BARBARA: Ahh . . . Well, I get self-righteous, and I judge her, and I get very uptight around it.

KATIE: And how does that feel, to live with no forgiveness?

BARBARA: It feels the hardest on myself. I'm pretty merciless on myself when I start condemning my sister. Merciless on her, and then merciless on me.

KATIE: **Who would you be without that thought,** without that lie— "She should listen to others"?

BARBARA: Well, I would have *her* in my life. I would be able to love her. I wouldn't feel this horrible resentment.

KATIE: Yes, honey. So with the thought, you feel angry and self-righteous and resentful—a lot of stress. And without the thought, you'd be able to love your sister. Can you see how it's your thoughts that are causing your suffering, not your sister?

BARBARA: Yes. That's pretty clear.

KATIE: The sister in your head is the one who is making you miserable. Your real sister may be living in agony and guilt over her decision. Who knows another person's mind? You love her, that's the problem. There's nothing you can do about that. These stories are just the attempt to keep you from experiencing your love, and it doesn't work, because you suffer from that. If I look out and tell the story of how anything is not love, I'm going to feel it as stress. That's how a lie feels. So let's **turn it around.**

BARBARA: I should listen to myself, and do what I think is the only way. Or do what I think is my way.

KATIE: Yes, and one way is just to call your sister and say, "I love you, and I'm working on my anger and sadness about Mom's death." Let her know what you found when you questioned your thoughts about her.

BARBARA: Hmm.

KATIE: Can you really know what your sister was going through during that week when she had your mother's life and pain in her hands?

BARBARA: I can't. I can't, but Laurie wasn't there with my mother. I was. Laurie was halfway across the country. She couldn't see her and hear her.

KATIE: And can you imagine what she was going through?

BARBARA: I'm sure there was a lot of pain, but I don't know what it was. I just can't imagine it.

KATIE: Exactly so. And when your mind is closed, you keep yourself from finding out. Close your eyes now, drop your story just long enough to look at your sister. Watch her trying to make her decision, a decision your mom trusted her to make, without superimposing your story onto her. What do you see?

BARBARA: It's hard for her.

KATIE: Yes, sweetheart. Now see if you can find another turnaround for that. "Laurie should listen to others."

BARBARA: I should listen to Laurie . . .

KATIE: Yes, honey.

BARBARA: . . . and do what she thinks is the only way. Oh, boy! That's a hard one.

KATIE: Pretty powerful.

BARBARA: We're both so stubborn. It would be amazing to be able to do that one.

KATIE: Yes. You know, it's the truth that sets us free. And you can find the truth only when you go inside. Going outside for a solution, trying to convince her to see it your way, is war. Fear is blind and deaf. Let's look at the next statement you've written.

BARBARA: *I need Laurie to stop being impatient with me.*

KATIE: **Is that true?** Is that what you need?

BARBARA: No, I don't . . . well . . . I think I do, but the truth is I know I'm stronger than that. I really don't need that.

KATIE: Isn't it wonderful to ask yourself? You could die believing that you need her to stop being impatient with you. And call it her fault—until you ask yourself. **How do you react when you believe that thought?** How do you treat her when you believe it?

BARBARA: I'm impatient.

KATIE: Yes. I am whatever I see you as in the moment.

BARBARA: I can see that.

KATIE: And how do you react when you believe the thought "I need Laurie to stop being impatient with me," and you're impatient?

BARBARA: I'm intolerant, I'm angry with her, I'm mean, I'm miserable.

KATIE: Yes, honey. Say more.

BARBARA: I'm depressed, I feel separate, resentful, powerless.

KATIE: **Who would you be without that thought,** which is not even true for you?

BARBARA: I would be calm, confident, not needing her to be any particular way. She could be impatient, and it wouldn't bother me at all.

KATIE: You would just be someone clear, stating what you want. And listening.

BARBARA: Yes. That would feel much better. That would be a much better way to be.

KATIE: Let's **turn it around.**

BARBARA: I need me to stop being impatient with me when I'm giving an opinion or feeling about something.

KATIE: So all this wonderful advice is for you to hear. Because she's not listening, haven't you noticed? There's another turnaround. "I need me . . ."

BARBARA: I need me to stop being impatient with Laurie when she's giving an opinion or feelings on something. That would be true, too.

KATIE: Yes, she was giving you every reason why she couldn't pull the plug. Were you listening?

BARBARA: No, I was just focused on my mom.

KATIE: And on what *you* wanted.

BARBARA: Well, that's true. You're right. And I was focused on my comfort level around it, too.

KATIE: That's okay, you know. This Work is not about a right or a wrong; it's about realizing for yourself what's true and moving on to kinder ways of acting. Because that's where freedom lies. Freedom from anger and freedom from resentment.

BARBARA: I really believed it was true that my mom should die when she wanted to die, because what I was seeing . . .

KATIE: And **is it true?**

BARBARA: She's telling me this.

KATIE: You bet. That's what she's telling you.

BARBARA: And what's true is that it's not happening.

KATIE: Exactly so. "Your mother knew when she should go." That doesn't ring true. The fact is that she handed over the power of decision to your sister.

BARBARA: So, even though her words and her face are indicating that it's true, it's just not true, because it's not happening.

KATIE: And there's a way you can talk to your mother and be in reality and at the same time totally loving. "Mother, I hear you, I hear what you want, and I'm going to do everything possible, and Laurie has the power of attorney. In the meantime, I am here to hold your hand and to do whatever is possible for you."

BARBARA: That's what I did.

KATIE: That's all you *could* do! But there are two ways to do that. One way is feeling powerless and resenting your sister, and the other way is simply available—loving your mother and loving your sister and listening to her as she makes that painful week-long decision.

BARBARA: The first one is much harder.

KATIE: Yes, because you had your plan. But reality has another.

BARBARA: Yes.

KATIE: You know, whenever I argue with reality, I lose. Reality is something I can trust. It rules. It is what it is, and once it is, there's nothing I can do to change it for the moment. Nothing. I love that! It's all so beautiful. I mean, we're breathing, then we're not, the sun rises, it shines, it sets, I love the clear air, I even love the smog. I spend a lot of my life in airports, and I breathe in a lot of jet fuel. How else can I die on time? Not one breath too soon or too late. There's a perfect order running. I'm a lover of what is. Who would I be without my story? Without my story, in this very moment, is where God and I are one. There's no separation, no decision or fear in it. It just knows. And that's who we are without our plans. "People should listen"—that's laughable! They don't until they do. Turn it around: *I* should listen. That's something I can work with. The rest is completely out of my hands.

BARBARA: Mmm.

KATIE: All those years I spent teaching and preaching to my children—I'm so grateful they didn't listen. [The audience laughs.] Let's look at the next one you've written. Read us your list.

BARBARA: Okay. So this is my list about Laurie. *Laurie is headstrong, stubborn, passionate, self-righteous, dynamic, intelligent, selfish, selfless, a bear of a mother, arrogant, caring, and kind.*

KATIE: Yes. So, sweetheart, **turn it around,** and see what that experience would be.

BARBARA: I am headstrong . . .

KATIE: "When it comes to Laurie, I am . . ."

BARBARA: When it comes to Laurie, I am headstrong, stubborn, passionate, self-righteous, dynamic, intelligent, selfish, selfless, a bear of a mother . . .

KATIE: ". . . a bear of a sister . . ."

BARBARA: A bear of a sister . . .

KATIE: ". . . and daughter . . ."

BARBARA: And daughter . . . arrogant, caring, and kind.

KATIE: Yes. Isn't that as true, or truer?

BARBARA: It could be. It could be.

KATIE: Which word was the most difficult for you to turn around to yourself?

BARBARA: "Selfless."

KATIE: Oh, honey. It's a life's work, isn't it? When Laurie's over there running her life, and you're mentally over there running her life, there's no one here for you.

BARBARA: Right. Yes.

KATIE: That's how loneliness is caused. That's the loss of yourself. When you're in her business, you're sisterless. You're mentally over there with her, judging her, telling her what she should have done, and you've left yourself.

BARBARA: Yes, it's true.

KATIE: That's what makes you feel separate and lonely. Losing one family member is enough. Let's look at your next statement.

BARBARA: Okay. *I don't ever want to be in the middle of someone's decision to die, and have to watch their agony because someone's late.*

KATIE: Yes. Now you may run this story over again in your mind.

BARBARA: I'm sure I will.

KATIE: So say, "I am willing . . ." and read it again. Really experience that willingness.

BARBARA: I'm willing to be in the middle of someone's decision to die, and have to watch their agony because someone is late.

KATIE: "I look forward to . . ."

BARBARA: I look forward to being in the middle of someone's decision to die and watching their agony because someone's late.

KATIE: Yes. And if that causes you resentment, sadness, or separation—anything less than love for your sister—write it down, put it on paper. All war belongs on paper. There's no nightmare you can't wake yourself up from. How many times have you played the story over in your mind since it happened?

BARBARA: Oh, thirty or forty times?

KATIE: Okay, thirty or forty times. And how many times did your mother die?

BARBARA: Well, she almost died three times over the last two months.

KATIE: Yes, and how many times did she die?

BARBARA: She actually died once, in agony.

KATIE: Yes, once. "She died in agony"—**is that true?**

BARBARA: I can't know that that's true. No.

KATIE: Absolutely. And **how do you react when you believe the thought** "My mother died in agony"?

BARBARA: I'm in agony about it. I see her face, I hear her words, or what I think she said, and I suffer a lot.

KATIE: So you can't know that your mother was really in agony, but you can know that you are in agony right now over her possible agony. And one person in agony is enough.

BARBARA: Yes.

KATIE: Can you see a peaceful reason to keep the thought "She died in agony"? I'm not saying she didn't die in agony. That's an ancient story. It's a religion. And I'm not telling you to drop it.

BARBARA: Actually, I don't think she did die in agony. I think that leading up to the actual dying, she at times appeared to be in agony.

KATIE: That's truer. She *appeared* to be in agony.

BARBARA: But I don't actually know.

KATIE: You are good, sweetheart.

BARBARA: I see her face and I hear her words, but . . .

KATIE: **How do you react when you believe the thought** that she died in agony?

BARBARA: Well, I feel helpless and inadequate and weak, because I couldn't give her what she wanted.

KATIE: **Who would you be without the thought?**

BARBARA: I would just be in witnessing her and helping her, loving her.

KATIE: Cherishing that week.

BARBARA: Oh, boy. Mmm. Okay.

KATIE: "My mother died in agony"—**turn it around.**

BARBARA: I died in agony?

KATIE: Yes. Over and over and over. You killed your joy in being with your mother during the last week of her life, your joy at witnessing the miracle of life as it moves on and begins again through you, with nothing to stop it. Oh, honey, it's enough agony. One person dying in agony is enough, and that one is you. We can't know about your mother, but *your* agony you can do something about. There's no nightmare you cannot wake yourself up from. That's not possible. Your story and reality just don't match. Reality is always kinder than your story about it—but only always.

BARBARA: Okay.

KATIE: I love what you found, honey. You think of her face, you hear her words, and I hear you say that you can't know she was in agony.

BARBARA: No, I can't know.

KATIE: Go to the place—and I invite everyone in the audience to go there—go to the place where you were in the most pain in your life. It could be emotional or physical pain, it doesn't matter. Go to that place. Can you find it? Where were you? What was going on? Can you find it?

BARBARA: Uh-huh.

KATIE: Are you there? Close your eyes. Now, in the middle of that experience, go to the place inside you where you understood, find the part of you that knew you were okay. Maybe in the most dramatic pain, you were even thinking something like "What's for dinner?" and all the while you're screaming on the floor. Go to that place. See if you can find it. [Pause.] You found it. Good, tell me.

BARBARA: Well, in that moment, watching my mother apparently suffering, I knew I didn't have any control over it, and I just came back to myself, and I felt, I'm okay right here, even though I'm watching something that's really hard, there's nothing I can do about it . . . and so I came back to me.

KATIE: Good, honey. And do you think your mother was any less wise or capable than you are? Sweetheart, we *all* have that place. We can all find it, if we look deeply enough, no matter how much pain we're in. It doesn't matter—that place is always there.

BARBARA: Yes, I think I probably underestimated her during that week.

KATIE: "I underestimated her during that week"—**turn it around.**

BARBARA: I underestimated myself during that week.

KATIE: Yes, honey. And you underestimated your sister.

BARBARA: All right.

KATIE: Oh, mothers are so beautiful. They die for us, can't you see? They die, as everyone does, so that we can come to understand. No mistake. And they die perfectly, in the way that's best for us. Would you choose that she died that way, if that were the only way you could find God?

BARBARA: Oh . . . [Pause.] Yes, I would.

KATIE: Yes, sweetheart. Well, that seems to be the case.

BARBARA: Thank you, Katie. I feel like such a burden has been lifted from me.

KATIE: You're welcome.

BARBARA [laughing]: And it will be interesting to call Laurie and tell her what I've found.

66

*All streams flow to the sea
because it is lower than they are.
Humility gives it its power.*

The material world is a metaphor of mind. Mind rises into its projections and must eventually come back to itself, just as streams flow back to the sea. No matter how brilliant the mind, no matter how large the ego that takes credit for its actions, when it comes to see that it doesn't know anything, that it *can't* know anything, it flows back to the origin and meets itself again, in all humility.

Once you realize what is true, everything flows to you, because you have become the living example of humility. The mind realized is content to stay in the lowest, least creative position. Out of that, everything is created. The lowest place is the highest place.

Less than a week after my return from the halfway house, word spread about my change, and strangers began calling me on the phone, asking me questions or asking if they could come see me. They would call me at all hours: in the middle of the night, all day long, often all night long—people from 12-step programs, people from the street, people from long distances away, people who had been told about me by the friend of a friend. What I heard in their questions was a longing. They would ask, "How can I find your freedom?" and I'd say, "I don't know. But if you want to see what it is, come live with me. All I know is that you're welcome to what I have."

There was a continuous stream of people coming to the house. One person would come, the phone would ring, then two more would show up, five, six, maybe a dozen by the evening. They had heard that I was a saint, a Master, a Buddha. They would say I had something called "enlightenment." I had no idea what that meant. It sounded like having the flu. When they looked at me with wonder in their eyes, I felt they were seeing me as some kind of freak, and that was okay with me. I knew I was free, but I was still being bombarded by all the delusions that humanity has ever suffered from. It didn't feel enlightened to me.

For about a year, I had to write down the beliefs that kept arising in my mind. I had to write them down and inquire, in order to hold reality firmly. They came very fast—hundreds, thousands of them. Each belief felt like a meteor crashing into a planet, trying to demolish it. Someone would say, or I would hear in my mind, "It's a terrible day," and my body would start to shake. It was as if I couldn't bear the lie. It didn't matter whether I or someone else spoke it, because I knew it was all me. The cleansing, the undoing, inside me was instantaneous, whereas when I offer inquiry to people, they're doing it in apparent time and space—in the density that looks like time and space. But for me, the timelessness was obvious. So, when a belief hit me, I would sit and write it down and put it up against the four questions and then turn it around. That first year, I was writing all the time, crying all the time. But I never felt upset. I loved this woman who was dying through inquiry, this woman who had been so very confused. I kept falling in love with her. She was irresistible.

Most mornings, before or after I went out walking, I would sit by a window in the sunlight and wait for an uncomfortable feeling to appear. If it did, I would be thrilled, because I knew that it was always the result of some thought I needed to clean up. I was this, too. So I would write the thought down, and there was a lot of humor in the process. The thoughts that I wrote down were almost always about my mother. I knew that if I burned through one delusion, I would burn through them all, because I was dealing with concepts, not with people. They were thoughts like "My mother doesn't love me"; "She loves my sister and brother more than me"; "She should invite me to family gatherings"; "If I tell the truth about what happened, she'll deny it and no one will believe me." That first year, it wasn't enough that a thought was being met by inquiry, wordlessly, in my mind. The thought had to be written down. You can't stop mental chaos, however motivated you are. But if you identify one piece of chaos and stabilize it, then the whole world begins to make sense.

So I'd write the thought down and question it. Sometimes I'd sit for an hour, sometimes for a whole morning and afternoon—however long it took to meet the thought with understanding. I could always see that the thought wasn't true, that it was an erroneous assumption. I could never find any proof that would hold up. And then I'd ask, "How do I react when I believe that thought?" and immediately I could see that *it* was the source of the potential suffering, not my mother. Then I would ask, "What was I before that thought? What would I be without it?" And I could also, so clearly, see the turnaround. I was dealing with cause-and-effect and polarities. I could see that one polarity was just as true as the other. "My mother doesn't love me": "My mother does love me." I was dying for a cause that had an equally true opposite. And nothing short of inquiry would stop the shaking.

I would put every concept about my mother on paper as I thought it, because those concepts were the most powerful for me. Then inquiry would clear them. I was working not with my own mother, but with the concepts that appear for every human being. We all have the same ones: "I want," "I need," "she should," "she shouldn't." I was engaged in the science of the self. I was mind realizing itself, God looking into its own mirror.

Humility is our natural response to seeing what's true about ourselves. When we judge others and question that judgment, then turn it around to ourselves, that is the fire and the purification. Our knees buckle, and we learn how sweet it is to lose—how that is the winning. That's what The Work is about. Some people call it forgiveness. I call it sanity.

67

Compassionate toward yourself,
you reconcile all beings in the world.

I notice that I fed myself this morning in the kindest way. The food was wholesome and simple, and if I hadn't had china and elegant flatware and chairs and table and candle, I would have found a place in the sun and sat and eaten breakfast with my hands. I wouldn't give myself less than the best of what is available at any moment. I love that I am my keeper, and I love what keeps the keeper: everything.

Making breakfast for Stephen and myself is about watching kindness in action. I watch it move to the refrigerator, a hand opens the door, and I call it mine. I can never believe that, and the mind song is the background music that I love. What will the hand reach for? It pulls out an egg carton and a loaf of bread, and I notice the light reflected off the white surfaces in the kitchen. The hand takes four eggs, the body moves to the counter, the hand puts two slices of bread in the toaster, takes out a fork, a bowl, cracks the eggs, scrambles them, adds salt and pepper, moves to the stove, puts a pat of butter in the skillet, watches it melt, pours in the eggs. And as they are cooking, I see mental pictures of chickens in the fresh air and sunlight (the eggs are free-range), and also pictures of chickens in cages on top of each other, being force-fed, and I ask myself where am I in a cage, and I wait in the silence. I see the long-ago times when I was in a cage, and what an endless, dark period that seemed to be, when I believed that my pain was unbearable even as I bore it, in that pitch-dark cage, with no way out. And then I saw the key, and I opened the door. And after that, every time a problem seemed to arise in this new world, it was like child's play, as if I were some kind of skilled magician, the sorcerer who makes everything disappear with one stroke of mind. All this as the eggs are cooking. To me, they are strength. They die so that I can live. I put them on two shiny white dishes, with the toast that has popped up in the toaster, and I move to the dining room table, where tea and teacups are waiting. What a beautiful word *breakfast* is. What a beautiful world.

Beyond what the mind can see is kinder than what it sees—that's the privilege of an open mind. Kindness resonates with the way things are. Kindness is sipping a cup of tea without the thought that I'm even sipping it. It's like being my own plant, feeling myself being watered, beyond any thought that that's what I even need. It's the sound of rain against the window, the gift of the sound of rain in my ears, the gift of life, which I did nothing to deserve. Kindness prepares what I am to eat in the next season. It even leaves a rainbow. It's infinite. It's the hair that protects my head in the sun, the ground that supports the floor. There's nothing that isn't kind. A death accomplishes what ordinary life could never do, letting you experience what is beyond identification: the bodiless self, mind infinitely free.

When you realize where you come from, no imagination can move you to believe that you are separate. Everything is seen for what it is, and you understand that no one is in danger of losing anything but his identification. And in that forever good news, in the face of everything that appears to be real, only kindness remains. It's nothing that can be taught. It's an experience; it's self-delight. When I give to you without motive, I am delighted. I act with kindness because I like myself when I do that. The kindness can only be to myself. It doesn't include anyone else, not even the apparent receiver. I am both giver and receiver, and that's all that matters.

The whole world belongs to me, because I live in the last story, the last dream: woman sitting in chair with cup of tea. I look out the window, and whatever I see is my world. There's nothing beyond that, not one thought. This world is enough for me. Anything I ever need to do or be is in this unlimited space. It's enough to accomplish my purpose, and my purpose is to sit here now and sip my tea. I can imagine a world outside what I can see, and as it happens I prefer this one. It is always more beautiful here, wherever I am, than any story of a future or a past. The here and now is where I can make a difference. It's what I live out of. Nothing more is required.

68

The best leader
follows the will of the people.

I follow the way of it, which is always revealed in the moment. It's God's will, and it's always crystal clear. When you no longer have a will of your own, there is no time and space. It all becomes a flow. You don't decide, you flow from one happening to the next, and everything is decided for you.

For the ten years before February 1986, I was depressed—for the last two, so deeply depressed that I could barely leave my bedroom. Every day I longed to die. I used to go for weeks at a time without brushing my teeth, because every time I thought of brushing my teeth, a belief would arise: "What's the use? It all adds up to nothing anyway." I was a dead woman, and why bother brushing your teeth when you're already dead? But after my mind became clear, if I was in bed and heard the voice say, "Brush your teeth," I would follow that, and nothing could stop me. I would get out of bed, I would *fall* out of bed if I had to, I would crawl on my belly into the bathroom, put the toothpaste on the toothbrush, and brush my damn teeth. I didn't care about cavities, I cared about one thing: honoring the truth inside me. Do you want to have an epiphany? Do you want to stand in front of the burning bush? Here's my burning bush: *Brush your teeth.*

To respect the way of it is to follow the simple directions. If you have the thought that the dishes need washing, wash them. That's heaven. Hell is asking why. Hell is "I'll do it later," "I don't have to do it," "It's not my turn," "It's not fair," "Someone else should do it," and on and on, ten thousand thoughts a minute. If it comes to you to do something, just do it. All the unquestioned thoughts about that action are how you hurt yourself. Doing what's next, without a mental argument, is devotion to God. It's a wonderful thing to just listen and obey, to listen and do. And if you follow the voice, you eventually realize that there's not even a voice. There is no voice, there's only movement, you *are* the movement, and you just watch it do itself. What comes next is not your business. You just move, and you undo every judgment you have about that. If it hurts, undo it.

It's April, and I'm on book tour, in Washington, D.C. A month ago, my doctor told me that I have osteoporosis and I need to walk more. More exercise, more calcium, a weekly pill, or my bones will crumble. I love his opinion. It amuses me, and I'm glad to follow his directions. When Stephen and I and our friend Adam arrive at the hotel, we're told that our rooms won't be ready until three o'clock. It's noon; there are three hours to go. Obviously now is the time to walk. How about near the Jefferson Memorial? The taxi drops us off at an intersection, and we start walking. Cherry blossoms! Everywhere we look, the most indescribably lovely blossoms. They are in full bloom—at their peak, we're told. Thousands of people have planned their vacations to be here at this precise moment. We had no idea about the cherry blossoms until suddenly there they were, in all their glory. Obviously the master plan was for us to see the blossoms in full bloom. My doctor's plan was for me to walk. The hotel's plan was to keep us from the rooms until they were cleaned. We could have gone through this experience with stories about how tired·we were after five weeks of nonstop traveling, how much we needed to rest, how inconsiderate of the hotel, what poor planning on the publicist's part, et cetera. But if our room had been ready, we would have missed the cherry blossoms. The way is clear, but only when the mind is clear.

Fast-forward to September. Ross's dog, Oakley, has jumped into the canal in front of my house. The French doors have been left open, and this big, simple-hearted golden retriever bolts through the doors, leaps the fence, and plunges into the water, in hot pursuit of ducks. The ducks don't seem to be too concerned; they look over to see who is making such a commotion, then paddle off, quacking, faster than he can swim. The next day, I see Oakley's muddy paw prints across the otherwise spotless floors, and my heart melts. As I clean the floors, the love that I experience for this animal is huge. I know what the prints are for. They connect me to my granddog and to my son and to the lightheartedness of the animal world, and I love that I am that. The unquestioned mind might see them and get upset, thoughts might attack the dog, attack my son for his lack of discipline, attack myself for not seeing the open doors sooner; there are thousands of combinations the mind might use to attack the apparent other in its quest to maintain body-identification. But the questioned mind sees no opposition. It delights in everything life brings.

My three-year-old twin granddaughters, Hannah and Kelsi, open the kitchen cupboard and pull out the most marvelous treasures, pots and pans and spoons, and the internal portion of a coffee press. Days later, I notice that the coffee press is still out. I love that they have left a piece of their curiosity and freedom behind. My house is very simply decorated; there's nothing extra. And now the coffee press. I love what it adds. You never know who your interior decorators are until they appear. And as I place the coffee press back in its old familiar position, hidden away under the counter, I don't miss it. The house is always decorated perfectly.

This morning I had the thought to shower, and I notice that I stayed with the e-mail. I find that fascinating. Showering was a wonderful idea. Will it move to that or not? It's exciting to wait and watch and allow life to move at its own pace as it continues to do what it does. For no reason, when a few dozen e-mails are finished, the body rises. Where is it going? It thinks it's going to the shower, but there's no way to know, not ever, until it's standing there in the shower stall, turning the knob. And until the water comes out, there is still no way to know if a shower will happen. As the water pours over my body, the thought arises, "What a wonderful idea!"

69

When two great forces oppose each other,
the victory will go
to the one that knows how to yield.

It's not possible for something to be against you. There's no such thing as an enemy; no person, no belief, not even the ego is an enemy. It's just a misunderstanding: we perceive something as an enemy, when all we need to do is be present with it. It's just love arising in a form that we haven't understood yet. And questioning the mind allows beliefs to simply arise. The quiet mind realizes that no belief is true, it is immovable in that, so there's no belief it can attach to. It's comfortable with them all.

Your enemy is the teacher who shows you what you haven't healed yet. Any place you defend is where you're still suffering. There's nothing out there that can oppose you. There is just fluid motion, like the wind. You attach a story to what you perceive, and that story is your suffering. I am everything that I have ever called other people; they were me all along. Everything I ever called my enemy was me. Projection would have us see reality as a them and a me, but reality is much kinder. All enemies are your kind teachers, just waiting for you to realize it. (And that doesn't mean you have to invite them to dinner.) No one can be my enemy until I perceive him as threatening what I believe. If there's anything I'm afraid of losing, I have created a world where enemies are possible, and in such a world there's no way to understand that whatever I lose I am better off without.

I return home after a trip, I open the door, and the house has been cleaned out. The burglars have taken my money, my jewelry, the television, the stereo, my CD collection, appliances, computers; they've left just the furniture and some clothing. The house has a clean Zen look. I go through the rooms and see that this possession is gone, that one is gone. There's no sense of loss or violation. On the contrary, I picture the recipients and feel what joy these items will bring them. Maybe they'll give the jewelry to their wives or lovers, maybe they'll sell it at a pawn shop and feed their kids with the proceeds. I am filled with gratitude. My gratitude comes from the obvious lack of need for each item. How do I know I don't need it? It's gone. Why is my life better without it? That's easy: my life is simpler now. The items now belong to the burglars, they obviously needed the items more than I did; that's how the universe works. I feel such joy for them, even as I fill out the police report. I find it odd that the way of the world is to try to retrieve what is no longer ours, and yet I understand it. Filling out the police report is also the way of it. If the items are found, I'm ready to welcome them back. And because they are never found, I understand that the shift in ownership is the best thing for the world, for me, and for the burglars. I need only what I have at any given time, never more, and never less. We can never have a problem with possessions; the only problem is our thoughts about what we do or don't possess. What other suffering is possible?

The simple truth of it is that what happens is the best thing that can happen. People who can't see this are simply believing their own thoughts, and have to stay stuck in the illusion of a limited world, lost in the war with what is. It's a war they'll always lose, because it argues with reality, and reality is always benevolent. What actually happens is the best that can happen, whether you understand it or not. And until you understand it, there is no peace.

Reality is always kinder than the story we tell ourselves about it. If I were to tell the story of reality, it would have to be a love story. The story would be told as life lives itself out, always kinder and kinder, with twists and turns that cannot be projected into the distance. For example, if my daughter dies, I realize that there is no self to be affected. It's not about me. This is about her life, my child's life, and I celebrate her freedom, because I know the freedom of unidentified mind—the unceasing bodiless mind that is finally awake to itself, the mind that never existed as a her, and the her that can never die. In this we are never separated. And that's just a beginning; it gets even kinder. I get to see what my child's children grow into because she was not there to teach them differently. Whenever I lose something, I've been spared. Every loss has to be a gain, unless the loss is being judged by a confused mind. I come to see what fills that space in my life because she isn't there. And because she lives in my heart, the kindness in my world cannot decrease, because something else enters the space that I held her in. Just when you think that life is so good that it can't get any better, it has to. That's a law.

I look at the leaf that has withered and gone crisp in its apparent lifelessness. The tree has had to let go of it as if it were nothing. It falls to the ground and begins to do its job, a different job now. It naturally does it, becomes mulch, becomes water and air. Eventually it becomes every element, it nourishes and becomes part of what makes the mother tree strong, substance and water and air and fire, everything doing its job in the moment it appears to be that. And again and again it lives the story of mind, the evolution of mind and what it projects as disservice in absolute service.

70

If you want to know me,
look inside your heart.

The mind open to being questioned is the only mind that can take this journey. The open mind is fearless in its quest to live without suffering. Eventually inquiry is easy to put into practice, because you learn to respect where your answers come from and the freedom they bring. And eventually the mind understands that it has found its desired path, the path leading home, back to its very own self, its ultimate resting place.

When the questions are asked and the answers are allowed to surface, the mind is often shocked at itself. It had no idea that such insights lived within it. And these answers allow deeper, more hidden answers to surface, to be seen and understood by the unknowing, inquiring polarity of mind. As mind comes to know its own nature, it begins to trust the wisdom that it is. This is its education, the end of all its suffering, delusion, fear, and mistaken identity. Inquiry changes the world faster than you can imagine. I was in a hurry. Now I walk as the questions, and I live as the answers. Because my intention was to be open, no matter what the consequences, I can't help but live in the world I call heaven. I even love my dentist.

At first, inquiry may seem more than you can handle; you may feel as if it is cutting your heart open without anesthesia. Everything you wanted to keep hidden comes to the surface, you feel all the repercussions of it, and you keep undergoing the death of who you thought you were. This may double you up; you may vomit or have temporary paralysis, for hours even. You are still identifying as a you, and you begin to see that you yourself are all the people you found unkind, brutal, stupid, crazy, greedy, despicable, and this is so painful that sometimes you don't think you can bear it. As it keeps inquiring, the mind continues to understand that it is its only enemy and that the world is entirely its projection, that it is alone, that there is no other, and that this is absolute. The turnarounds always keep it grounded with the invitation of being human. This balance sustains it between nothing and something, gives it the solid ground of a world, and allows trust to grow as you continue, sweetly and surely, to dissolve what is left.

At some point, because it has become completely rooted in itself, identity is lost as anything but mind. It cannot be anything other than that again. It is dead to anything else. There can be grief, the experience of terrible loss, and loneliness, when mind loses its identification as human, and at this point it may begin to find other identities, terrifying identities: a bird when you don't know how to fly, a rock when you're in a hurry, and you can only sit there forever, knowing that eventually you'll turn to dust, and until then you're there, with no arms, no legs, merely a rock. But with the power of inquiry, you love that you're that, you don't desire any other identity, and then you realize that you can't have even that, there's no identification that you can live as, only mind. And as mind, you discover that every thought is gone, and only a thought that says it existed is left as its proof, and that's gone, too, and in this, all thought is gone, everything is already gone—everything.

Inquiry continues to kill what you think you are, until you discover something else. The questioned mind is pure wisdom, and it can heal the whole world. As it heals, the world heals. I came to see that I couldn't live until I died. And what lives, thank God, is not the me I thought I was. There is nothing I am that is not beautiful. I appear as all things, the old and the new, the beginning and the end. I'm everything. I'm you.

You can go anywhere, and where you are in the moment shows this to be true. You *are* anywhere. What would this place be without a name? Magical, sacred, miraculous. How did you get here? Why would you need a destination? It only turns out to be this or that anyway, what you planned or what you didn't plan. I understand that you love when your plan matches reality, and in all of that, here you are now, as the future you always wondered about, on the street, checking out the garbage bin for any delight, noticing that it's all beyond what you really need, beyond what you already have in this moment, from your lavish home, as you sit at your dining room table, looking at the excess, everything that you don't need, depriving yourself in your mind of what is already so full within you in this moment now. Without your story, aren't you fine? Isn't life's own destination more wondrous than imagination could dictate?

What is adversity? It's simply when your story doesn't match reality. Suppose the story is "I am the man who will live out his life with two arms; the knife will be in my right hand and the fork in my left," and in reality my right arm is gone. All of a sudden, I wake up, it's gone, and I didn't even get to say good-bye—it's in a plastic bag in the trash bin in the backyard. Now I am the man with a fork in the right hand, and the right hand turns out to be my left. So reality isn't being matched by my story, the identity I hold so dear. It has its own story to be lived out. I can be the man who loves learning what is new, the man who can't cut the steak, and I can love the vegetarian I notice I'm becoming. I am always what I believe myself to be, until I question my thoughts and come to understand that reality is what I am, and that it is always kinder than the identity I'm trying to hold on to.

Grace means understanding that where you are is where you always wanted to be. It means losing that arm and noticing what remains, in full appreciation and gratitude, and seeing at the same time how much better off your life is without the arm, and all the benefits that this new way brings. It's the realization that where you are and what you are and what everything is and how it is, in every moment, is your heart's desire, fulfilled beyond what you ever could have imagined.

71

Not-knowing is true knowledge.

To think you know something is to believe the story of a past. It's insane. Every time you think you know something, it hurts, because in reality there's nothing to know. You're trying to hold on to something that doesn't exist. There is nothing to know, and there is no one who wants to know it.

It's so much easier to know that you don't know. It's kinder, as well. I love the don't-know mind. When you know that you don't know, you're naturally open to reality and can let it take you wherever it wants to. You can drop your identity and be who you really are, the unlimited, the nameless. People call me "Katie," but I don't ever believe it.

Someone says, "I'll be here at nine o'clock." No one can know what it's like for someone with no future to watch a clock become nine. The event is so miraculous that there are no possible words for it. It's one minute past eight, then suddenly it's two minutes past eight, according to a clock that is always pointing to now. And now it's eight-thirty, and now, all at once, it's nine, and the person shows up—just pops out of nowhere—from a past that doesn't exist. I am in continual amazement at such happenings.

Now I am walking to the living room, I think. I think that I'm on my way to open the window. I have no clue where it's actually going;

I don't know if the window even exists, or if there is such a thing as a living room. As body moves, I hear each step on the hardwood floor as if it were mine: this step, then the next, then the next. I experience everything in slow motion. More accurately, I experience everything frame by frame by frame. Each moment is a frame for me, not necessarily connected with any other. It's like the rock with lichen on it that you look at through a magnifying glass: a universe in itself, completely undivided. When I'm walking, each movement within one step is complete in itself. It's one step at a time, but actually it's everything in between that, too. Now. Now. Now. There is literally no time and space, no past or future, not even a present, no one coming, no one going, no meaning to it, no motive, no goal. And finally you get to a place where nothing moves. That is home, the place we all long for, the still point, the center of the universe, absolute zero.

Miraculously, the living room appears, a window appears, and I experience a little girl's excitement, spilling over like a bubbly artesian wonderment. Will it go to the window? That's what seems to be happening, and I can never know, as I feel its next step, body moving forward, the click of a shoe. Will it open the window? Is that the way of it? I notice a hand reaching out, and as the phone rings, I experience a burst of internal laughter as the body turns to walk in the other direction. This is the only way the window could stay closed, and a window that is closed now is the way of it. I see a hand pick up the phone, just because it does, and again I delight in the way of it. Lips move, voice speaks into the phone—"Hello"—and I am thrilled at the familiar sound out of nowhere, its very own voice, this endless, mindless, ecstatic dream of what isn't, with no meaning, no sorrow, no life, no death. There is nothing about it that is not the *is,* and therefore nothing that is not beautiful.

I watch as my body moves to the kitchen, to the stove. I watch as my hand picks up the steamer and takes the journey to the sink. You never know what it will do until it does it. Will it eat the squash from the steamer? It takes a plate from the cupboard and puts a piece of squash onto it. And it is the squash, it is the steam rising from it, it is the body, the plate, the sink, the counter. And what am I? I must be a . . . a what? I can't find an identity, as everything else is busy being what it is. Is it really necessary to be something? No, and also that's not possible. Can I pretend to be something? No: too late. My time for that is past, I'm awake as nothing but laughter, inner lightning, aware, alive in myself, and not this, not this, not this. The squash gets to be a something, the sink gets to be a something, and yet I can never be anything, no matter how much I might attempt to create myself as substance. I can imagine colors, sounds, as I create squash, counter, plate, and notice again that this dream, too, which is constantly disappearing, gone even as I notice it, is as vibrant as the dream of window or phone. It lives only for its own delight, is only a flash in apparent time. Will it use a fork? Its hands? I watch the dream; I love it. Even as I notice it eating the squash, the squash cannot exist. Taste? I don't bother projecting it, since it projects without me. It is delicious, and the taste is dreamed, the squash is dreamed, the counter, plate, and fork are dreamed, and the dreamer, too, is dreamed. And I notice that this is all I can be and that everything is born out of me and there is nothing that is or isn't. It's all one huge, amazing joke. If I could smile, I would.

72

When they lose their sense of awe,
people turn to religion.

A Christian asked me if I had ever met Jesus. I'm a lover of God—in other words, a lover of reality. I like to meet you there, which is here, now.

I don't know much about Jesus, except that he loved God. He was a man with a wonderful way that worked for him—someone who truly lived it. I know what that is. I found a wonderful way, too, and I live it. And, of course, that's not true. "I" didn't find the way, it found me, when there wasn't even a me to find. The way is simply what is. It doesn't bend to what anyone thinks it should be, it is its own integrity, it is infinitely intelligent and kind. To my mind, if Jesus is the way, I meet him in everyone, because the way is nothing more than a mirror image of my own thinking.

Christians say they love Jesus, but that's easy to believe when things are going your way. If Jesus walked into this room, everyone would love him, some would even fall at his feet and worship him, until he said something that threatened their religion, which is the concept they're attached to in the moment. Then he'd become an enemy. "He's a radical. He's not what I thought he'd be. He hangs out with the wrong people. A spiritual teacher shouldn't be political. He's contradicting the scriptures. His head's in the clouds. He doesn't understand." People will write off even the clearest, most loving person in the world when he opposes their belief system. They will invalidate him, negate him, obliterate him, prove that he's wrong, he's a fraud, he's dangerous to society, so that they can protect what they really believe is important. They'd rather be right than free.

When you revere a spiritual teacher, it's yourself that you're revering, because you can't project anything but yourself. And as long as there is something unhealed in you, you have to attach that to the teacher when you don't get your way or when your belief system is threatened. He says something, you put meaning onto it, you think that he's wrong or lacking, and you move out of reverence. What you're reacting to is not what he said, but what you heard. It's a fine thing to love Jesus, but until you can love the monster, the terrorist, the child molester, until you can meet your worst enemy without defense or justification, your reverence for Jesus isn't real, because each of these is just another of his forms. That's how you know when you are truly revering your spiritual teacher: when your reverence goes across the board.

If you think you're devoted to a spiritual teacher, that's a wonderful beginning; you get to see how your devotion could look when it's directed to all of us. Whatever disrespect, invalidation, or fear you project onto an enemy—sooner or later you'll project it onto your spiritual teacher. Everyone is your teacher, and the most powerful spiritual practice is to hang out with the people who criticize you. You don't even have to do that physically, since they live right here in your head. And when you think that you've grown beyond all your defensiveness and justifications, then hang out with your enemies physically, and see how lighthearted you are when they trash you. That's the real test.

To become aware without any spiritual teacher, without any scripture or tradition or authority, is to meet the teacher where you are. For me, the truth was right under my nose. Most amazing. It was sweet and simple, with nothing complicated about it. If it hadn't been so simple, I would never have found it.

73

The Tao is always at ease.

The balanced mind is always at ease. It isn't for or against any-thing; it only wants what is. It's at ease because there's nothing it is opposed to. Nothing opposes it, nothing holds it back, it acts as creation unfolding in the moment, and its action is swift and free.

It's not attached to pleasure, because it doesn't need more than it has already. Usually pleasure is a subtle form of discomfort, because even as you're enjoying sex or food, for example, you cling to your enjoyment; you want it to last, you want more of it, or you're afraid of losing it even as it's happening. The difference between pleasure and joy? Ohhh . . . the distance is from here to the moon—from here to another galaxy! Pleasure is an attempt to fill yourself. Joy is what you are.

Once you understand yourself, you are the pleasure you were seeking; you are what you always wanted. Pleasure is a mirror image of what you already have before you look away from what really is. When you stop seeking, the beauty concealed by the seeking becomes evident. What you wanted to find is what remains, beyond all stories.

When you no longer believe your thoughts, you experience pleasure with a feeling of gratitude and joy, because there's no control in it. The taste of broccoli—what could be more enlightening than that? Or sex—it's the epitome of letting go, surrendering to God, which is another name for reality. When sex is without control, you have no idea what can happen. An orgasm can be so intense and last so long that you feel it's going to kill you. But because there's nothing that you can attach to, you give yourself to it completely.

For twenty years I haven't met a story I didn't love. If you're having the most beautiful dream, would you want someone to wake you up? I love my happy dream: "This is a perfect world. People are kind. God is good." But if you're having a nightmare, you may want to wake yourself up, though it will cost you your suffering.

Many spiritual paths, I'm told, take a stand against pleasure. But life becomes difficult when you are against anything. It's painful to have an enemy. It's the war with the self. Thoughts are friends, they're part of reality, and until you deeply see that not even thoughts are real, you'll spend your whole life struggling against them.

Love is the power, and the beautiful dream is nothing more than a clear mirror image of love. All identification is felt within that. It's felt as a balance and celebration of its true nature. And, true or not, it is balanced. All the pain we have ever suffered, all the pain that any human being on this planet has ever suffered, is over in this present moment. We live in a state of grace.

74

If you realize that all things change,
there is nothing you will try to hold on to.

Babies aren't born into the world of illusion until they attach words to things. When you're clear, it's great fun to observe that. I love being with my grandbabies, I love hearing what I teach them: "That's a tree." "That's a sky." "I love you." "You're Grandma's precious angel." "You're the most beautiful baby in the world." All these lies, and I'm having a wonderful time telling them. If I'm creating problems for my grandchildren, they can question their stressful thoughts when they grow up. I am joy. I'm not going to censor any of it.

Every story we tell is about body-identification. Without a story, there's no body. When you believe that you are this body, you stay limited, you get to be small, you get to see yourself as apparently encapsulated in one separate form. So every thought has to be about your survival or your health or your comfort or your pleasure, because if you let up for a moment, there would be no body-identification. Every thought has to be about "I"—that's how you survive. And then, as soon as you get your little piece of turf, your little house, your little car, your thoughts turn to the story of how you need to be healthy and comfortable. You get stuff in the shopping cart, you get stuff in the house, and as soon as you're comfortable, your thoughts turn to pleasure. This is full-scale body-identification: there's no thought that isn't about the body. So you go to pleasure when you have all your little ducks in order. And all pleasure is pain, until you understand.

Your body is not your business. If you're sick, go to your doctor. That way you get to be free. Your body is your doctor's business; *your* business is your thinking, and in the peace of that, you're very clear about what to do. And then the body becomes a lot of fun, because you're not invested in whether it lives or dies. It's nothing more than a metaphor for your thinking, mirrored back to you.

When I was in Amsterdam several years ago, I did The Work with people from early morning till late at night, even though I was running high fevers. And I noticed that a few times, during a break, I would be huddled up in a corner, exhausted, shaking, in heaven. The shaking was fine with me, and the exhaustion. I was just there to do my job, in sickness or in health, for richer or for poorer. And, in the clarity of that, I always seem to be well. No story, no sickness. There was snow, there was cold, there was sky, there were people, there was breath, there was fever, there was exhaustion, there was joy—everything! Without a story, I'm free.

I once went for twenty-seven days without food. There was no reason for it—I just knew not to eat. And during all those days I couldn't find a trace of hunger. Hunger was just another myth. My family and friends were fearful for my life, but I wasn't concerned; I felt healthy and strong; the whole time, I was doing a lot of vigorous walking in the desert. And at no moment did I experience anything but myths about hunger and bellyaches and weight loss. I couldn't find one legitimate need that didn't come face-to-face with the fear of death. And then, after twenty-seven days, for no reason, I ate.

If you don't identify as a body, the mind may occasionally find itself as a galaxy or a rock or a tree or a moon, a leaf, a bird. It may identify anywhere in the vastness of itself. I am this? I am this? To be a human is no more and no less important than to be a rock or a speck of dust. It's all equally important, all the same thing. It's limitless. It's still. It's what we all are without a story or a particular body-identification to believe in.

When you dream, you are the whole dream and everything in it. You have to be: you're the dreamer. You're bodiless, you're free—you're a man, you're a woman, a dog, a tree, you're all of it simultaneously; you're in the kitchen one moment and on a mountaintop the next; you're in New York and suddenly you're in Hawaii; nothing is ever stable because you can't body-identify; there's no identification you can attach to. That's how unlimited the mind is when there's no particular body to be.

Without a story of being limited, you're infinite. There's nothing more joyous than that—to know that you're all things and new each moment, and that all of it is projected. People think that limitlessness is terrifying, because they don't have inquiry. But it's no more terrifying than sitting in your living room. It's exactly the same after the initial experience. The ego does everything not to let an experience like that happen. If the experience does happen, the ego body-identifies at a higher level, to hold on to what it thinks it knows. It tries to control body-identification so that it can make sure such experiences never happen again. For people who don't have inquiry, the ego may say, "There's no way back," and then the thought may be "I'm going insane." But if inquiry is alive in you, you can't attach to any frightening thought. It doesn't matter if you're a Katie or a bird or a galaxy or a rock or a tree or a grain of sand.

Eventually there is no fear. You come to feel total acceptance: "I am this, for now." And it's all okay. I'm only here with you in this moment. I'm an old woman the next. I'm a seagull the next. For hundreds of years I'm a redwood tree. Now I'm a mosquito, now a speck of dust, now a star that has just been born and will burn out billions of years from now. Time is irrelevant. I give myself to whatever the reality of it may be.

These apparent transformations aren't transformations at all. *It* is always what it is, beyond identification, aware of itself, delighted with itself, as all things. In this infinite loving state, it shoots out to know, to revel in its identities, to see what it hasn't yet revealed to itself. And in each experience, you realize that you're nothing; you're prior to thought, not a woman or a bird or anything but awareness: a completely silent mind looking out—in—gratefully, at itself.

75

Act for the people's benefit.
Trust them; leave them alone.

I trust everyone. I trust them to do what they do, and I'm never disappointed. And since I trust people, I know to let them find their own way. The wonderful thing about inquiry is that there's no one to guide you but you. There's no guru, no teacher who, in her great wisdom, shows you the answers. Only your own answers can help you. You yourself are the way and the truth and the life, and when you realize this, the world becomes very kind.

When my daughter, Roxann, attended her first workshop with me, it was in 1993, with a large group of therapists present. She was working on "the mother from hell"—which was how she had experienced me sometimes as she was growing up. She couldn't bear to look at me as she was doing her Work; it was hard for her even to hear the sound of my voice. I was the root of her problem, she thought, and I was also her salvation; she had to ask the monster for help, which made her furious. At a certain moment she became very passionate and got right in my face and said I should have mothered her differently. I said, "That's not my job. Mother yourself, honey. *You* be the mother you always wanted." Later she told me that that was the greatest gift I ever gave her. It turned out to be her freedom. I know the privilege of mothering myself. It's hopeless to see it as anyone else's job. Here's what I've told all my children: "You have the perfect mother. I'm responsible for all your problems, and you're responsible for the solutions."

Ultimately there is only you: you are your own suffering, you are your own happiness. What you give is what you receive, and I love that. I am always receiving for myself what I give to others. *Sacrifice* is not a word that holds any meaning for me, since, in my experience, giving something away doesn't—can't—mean giving it up. When I give it to you, it's me I'm giving it to. There's no separation.

Yesterday a young woman spent five minutes telling me how beautiful and kind and wise I am. Her face was flushed with the joy of telling me; she was in love with her story of Byron Katie. As I listened, looking into her eyes, I didn't need to say, "Turn it around," because that was automatically happening in me. Everything she said about me I was seeing in her, since I can only be her reflected image. Through her thoughts, I was seeing who *she* was; it was her own nature she was describing. If she had told me the sad story that I've heard from others so many times—"I'm lost, I'm miserable, nothing makes sense, I'm not good enough, life is unfair, how could he do that to me?"— I would have sat without any sadness or concern, since I know that on the deepest level everyone realizes that it's all untrue. When someone tells a sad story, I hear a mind that believes that it believes what is not, and I am touched by the impossible attempt to make the unreal real. In this I experience my own mind again, and I feel just as joyful as when I sit with the happy, adoring, adorable young woman of yesterday.

Expectation and no expectation are the same. I expect anything to happen, and it does. I expect nothing to happen, and ultimately I'm always right. Nothing has ever happened but a thought. I expect you to love me, and however you act toward me, however you feel, the fact is that you always love me. You may think that you don't, but you can't not love me. Thoughts seem to block this awareness, and if they're stressful, I invite you to question them and set yourself free.

The awakened mind is its own universe. There's nothing outside it. (Delightedly, there's nothing inside it, either.)

When mind projects as another, it only meets itself again. There can never be two. Someone says, "Hello, Katie, it's a wonderful day." How benevolent the way of it, that it would greet itself like this, out of nowhere. Someone else says, "It's a terrible day," and the mind leaps with joy in the pure experience of itself. The I-know mind, the mind that seems to suffer, the awesome, dear, humorous trickster, will challenge the wisdom and sanity of its balanced self, as it continues to wake up. But ultimately there is no separation. Every thought makes up the world of what it names joy, lightheartedness, inclusion, goodness, generosity, rapture, and (my favorite term) friendship. Ultimately, mind becomes its own friend.

76

The soft and supple will prevail.

All things change, because perception is constantly changing. When your mind is enlightened to itself and you notice that the world is a reflection of your own thinking, you're never surprised at these changes. You become supple, you discover that you can delight in change, you see the goodness of creation and how it can only keep surpassing itself. Why would the mind hold on to what was, when it recognizes that what is is always better?

I have a new inner cornea, thanks to my wonderful trailblazer genius surgeon, Dr. Mark Terry. The transplant surgery in Portland was an extraordinary success: thirty-nine hours afterward, my right eye had 20/30 vision (the surgery is considered successful if the patient has 20/100 vision after a week). Now, a month later, it's 20/20. I can read very small print, and what I see is sharp, clear, colorful—a world I haven't known in a very long time. No more pain, no more blindness and near-blindness in the right eye. The transplant surgery for the left eye is scheduled for two months from now.

What a thrill to walk around with someone else's (is it true?) cornea! I can't describe the miracle of being given unnecessary sight, and the joy of loving the always-more-than-I-need abundance of reality. Without my husband, the surgery probably wouldn't have happened, since I was perfectly happy with two corneas like smogged-up windowpanes. I see everything I need to see, with or without eyesight. It's a world in which, like everyone else, I always look beautiful and perfect. If I have eye makeup on my chin and breakfast on my sweater, how would I know? And where is the problem, other than in someone else's mind? Stephen did all the research and totally was the desire for my vision, and I am so grateful for his mind's creation, this clear, crisp world that doesn't cloud over, this absence of pain. And I am so grateful to the donor and the donor's family.

Believing that what you want equals what's best for you is a dead end. It makes the mind stiff, inflexible, caught in a picture of reality, rather than open to the wisdom of the way of it. What is is immovable, and it's constantly changing, it flows like water, it has as many supple, beautiful forms as the mind can create—an infinity of forms— and inside them all, behind them all, it just waits. The heart doesn't move, it just waits. You don't have to listen to it, but until you do, you're going to hurt. And the heart says only one thing: "What is is." As you do The Work, you return to the place you never actually moved from, the heart, the sweet center of the universe. *Heart* is just another name for the open mind. There is nothing sweeter.

77

The Master can keep giving
because there is no end to her wealth.

We think that because Jesus and the Buddha wore robes and owned nothing, that's how freedom is supposed to look. But can you live a normal life and be free? Can you do it from here, right now? That's what I want for you. We have the same desire: your freedom. And I love that you're attached to material objects, whether you have them or not, so that you can come to realize that all suffering comes from the mind, not the world.

A material thing is a symbol of your thinking. It's a metaphor for desire, for "I want," "I need." We don't have to give up our things. They come or go; we have no control over that; we may think we do, but in reality we don't. Whoever started teaching that we need to get rid of things, or even to give them all away, was a little confused. We may notice sometimes, after the fact, that if we lose everything we're much freer, so we think that it's better to live without possessions. And then we notice that we're not free anymore. But when we work with our thoughts, having great wealth equals having no possessions. A mind that loves reality is the only freedom.

Abundance has nothing to do with money. Wealth and poverty are internal. Whenever you think that you know something and it feels stressful, you're experiencing poverty. Whenever you realize that what you have is enough and more than enough, you're rich.

For people who enter the inner world, the world of inquiry, jobs become secondary. Your job is not about making money, or working with people, or impressing your friends, or getting respect, or having security. It's a place for you to judge, inquire, and know yourself. Everything—every man, woman, and child, every tree, every stone, every hurricane, every war—is about your freedom. Jobs come and go, companies and nations rise and fall, and you're not dependent on that. Freedom is what we all want; it's what we already are. And once you understand, you can be as excellent, as creative as you like in your job, you can give all your energy to it, because there's no longer any possibility of failure. You realize that the worst that can happen is a thought.

Money is not your business; truth is your business. The story "I need more money" is what keeps you from realizing your wealth. Whenever you think that your needs are not being met, you're telling the story of a future. Right now, you're supposed to have exactly as much money as you have right now. This is not a theory; this is reality. How much money do you have? That's it—you're supposed to have exactly that amount. If you don't believe it, look at your checkbook. How do you know when you're supposed to have more? When you do. How do you know when you're supposed to have less? When you do. Realizing this is true abundance. It leaves you without a care in the world, as you look for a job, go to work, take a walk, or notice that the cupboard is bare.

The heart can sing, can't it! That's why you wanted money in the first place. Well, you can skip the money part, and just sing. It doesn't mean you won't have money too. Can you do it for richer or poorer, as the world sees it?

I love having money, and I love not having it. To me, spending money is nothing more than passing on what didn't belong to me in the first place. There's nothing I can do to keep it away, as long as it needs to be passed on. If it doesn't need to be passed on, there's no need for it to come. I love that it comes in, and I love that it goes out.

When I receive money, I am thrilled, because I'm fully aware that it's not mine. I'm just a channel, I'm not even the caretaker. I get to be the observer of it, to see what it's for. The moment I get it from over there, a need for it pops up over here. I love giving money. I never lend people money; I *give* them money, and they call it a loan. If they repay it, that's when I know it was a loan.

78

Therefore the Master remains
serene in the midst of sorrow.
Evil cannot enter her heart.
Because she has given up helping,
she is people's greatest help.

The awakened mind is like water. It flows where it flows, envelops all things in its path, doesn't try to change anything, yet in its steadiness all things change. It goes in and out, around and over, above and below, and without meaning to, it penetrates wherever it can. It delights in its own movement and in everything that allows or doesn't allow it. And eventually everything allows it.

An old friend perceives me as unkind. He has all the proof. And though I am not the person he knew twenty-five or thirty years ago, he must continue to project his experiences of the old me onto the woman in front of him now. For the last twenty years he has continued to meet that woman of his thoughts, yet the woman of today is like water. I don't move back, I don't avoid, I don't attempt to change his mind, I don't defend or qualify, I listen to him as a student while he tells his story of me, I continue to flow in and out, over and under and around, always listening, looking into his eyes, and loving him. And today, for the first time, I noticed that when he talked about me he seemed lighthearted and trusting. As we walked to the park, he took my hand. We sat under a tree, and he told me what was going on in his inner life. It was such an intimate conversation. He seemed to have caught up to me, as if he were seeing and responding to something other than his old projection. It was as if I were watching myself reborn in him, and he was sitting with someone we both knew: a friend. I got to hear about his sorrow and his happiness, rather than about the woman who didn't exist, the one who had caused his problems. There was a lot to laugh about this time, and I sat with two of us who were like water, flowing together, joined as one. It wasn't the water that had changed, it was the rock. And in that change, the water continues to flow.

At the beginning, in 1986, I felt a lot of surprise that people were confused at what I was trying to express, that they believed that the separations they saw were real. This went on for about a year. I would cry a lot. It was like a dying. The tears were tears of amazement that people didn't understand that all suffering is imagined. I was moved by their innocence. It was like watching babies hurting themselves, like watching the innocent cut themselves with knives, with no possibility that they could stop. I didn't dare say, "This is unnecessary," because that would have been just another dagger in them.

And always the tears were tears of wonder and gratitude. I remember the first time someone brought me a cup of tea, I just melted with the splendor of it all. I had never seen a cup of tea before. I didn't know that we did that here. The man poured the tea, and my eyes began to overflow like the tea he was pouring. It was so beautiful, and there was such generosity in it. I felt so much love that I could only die into it, and just keep dying. There was no way to contain it, it was so huge. The tea poured in, an act of pure kindness, and the tears poured out of me in the same measure, received and pouring back, given back to itself, not to anyone or from anyone. And no one could understand why I was sobbing. They all thought I was sad. There was no way I could explain how moved I was, and that it was gratitude that was pouring out of me.

The Master has given up helping because she knows there is no one to help. And since she loves and understands her own nature, she realizes that in every action she is serving herself and sitting at her own feet. So there is nothing she gives that she doesn't receive in the same motion, as the same internal experience. Even when she appears not to give, that is what she is giving. The Master is the woman who dented your car, the man who stepped in front of you on line at the supermarket, the old friend who accused you of being selfish and unkind. Do you love the Master yet? There's no peace until you do. This is your work, the only work, the work of the Master.

79

Failure is an opportunity.

It's impossible to fail at anything. Your success just may not look the way you thought it would. If your goal was to go from point A to point C, for example, and you went from point A to point B, that's not a half-success—it's a complete success. If you can go all the way to C, good. Don't we love it when our dream comes true? But if you get only halfway, there's no sane reason to think you failed at that task. It's your job to open your mind and realize why it's better to have gotten to B than to C. In life, there's a sweeter dream than yours: reality. That's the ultimate dream, the kindest dream. We don't know where we're going, we just like to imagine that we know. I never believe it. That way, wherever I am, my journey is complete and I'm a success, because here I am.

Our nature is goodness. I know that's true because any thought that sees something as not good feels like stress. I can't be rejected; that's not possible. If someone says, "I don't want to be with you," I think, *How wonderful! He's showing me whom not to be with.* I don't take it personally. I remember when I didn't want to be with me, either, so I can appreciate his feeling and join him there. And I understand that the reason he doesn't want to be with me is that he believes what he thinks about me. He can't help it, because he hasn't questioned his mind.

Every time you think you have failed, you're identifying as a failure. And every time this identification arises, other thoughts surface that attempt to prove it. That's how the confused mind stays confused, how mind allows itself to live in the illusion of a past that never existed. If someone said, "Katie, you failed to answer my e-mail," I would laugh to myself and think, *Well, of course. There's no other way for me to succeed at being me.* (And then I might say, "Tell me what your e-mail was about.")

I took a test in a women's magazine. I was waiting in a hair salon, the magazine caught my eye, and I opened it at random. The headline said, HOW GOOD A LOVER ARE YOU? There was a page full of questions. *Do you prepare for his arrival?* No. *Do you put on sexy lingerie?* No. *Do you try special techniques to please him?* No. I added up my numbers at the end and discovered I had flunked the test. I loved that. To their mind, I am a dud. To my mind, I'm the perfect lover. Why would I prepare for his arrival? How could I project anything better than Stephen? And why would I bother? He is all I want when he walks in the door, and in every moment. Do I wear sexy lingerie? That might be fun, and I notice that the thought never occurs to me. I also notice that it's unnecessary. Do I have special techniques to please him? Why would I try to please him? He is already pleased, and I did nothing for it. What were these editors thinking?! Love is not a doing, nor is making love. Who needs props or techniques when the heart is wide open? The real plan is always the way of it, eliminating the need for any plan I might have. I don't know a thing about pleasing or being pleased. So there's no way I can't be the perfect lover.

80

If a country is governed wisely,
its inhabitants will be content.

I am content doing the thing in front of me, since my mind doesn't conflict with what I do. It has no reason to; there are no beliefs that would get in the way. Because the world is internal, I don't search for anything outside. Everything outside is inside. I have no need to meet anyone other than the people who enter my life, so my life is a continual invitation. I invite everyone and everything to come and go as they wish; all experiences are welcome here. There is never anything alien to the mind at peace with itself. It is its own joyous community.

I get up at 4:00, and notice the warmth that I rise out of, the pillows, the rumpled sheets, the sleeping body of my husband, this body rising, and as I walk to the bathroom, I notice the substanceless-ness of it all, the dream of where I am standing now in front of the sink, and I notice that as I stand, I am literally being born right now into this unknowing. Just because I call it a wall, a mirror, or a ceiling doesn't make it that. It's something more beautiful than any word could imply. Reality is continual creation in the moment, brilliant in its simplicity. The delighted onlooker that I am watches it go to the toilet, brush its teeth, walk down the stairs, brew its tea, sit down, as if it were a puppet with no puppeteer. What will it do next? It sinks into a corner of the couch, becomes the woman drinking the tea, and the woman becomes as still as the wall or the ceiling. And it notices the woman being breathed, in and out, a finger being moved ever so slightly, and I am the cup, the tea, the lips of the woman, I am the tea in the darkness, flowing down through the throat and into the belly, flowing through the system that is so dark and endless, and never projecting its end, always following and open to whatever could be better than this, and now I am nothing, and now I am a pond, and now I am nothing, and now I am a cloud, and now I am the rain, and now I am again gardening, watering, becoming this tomato, this carrot, this cell, this human body, this no-body, this nothing that is its origin, its end, its joy.

81

The more she does for others,
the happier she is.
The more she gives to others,
the wealthier she is.

Once, standing in front of a large audience, I realized that I didn't ever have to speak again—not then, not ever. I knew that no force on earth could prompt a word from my mouth, that there was nothing to say, and that words were absolutely unnecessary. So I just stood there and waited, fascinated to see what would come next. Finally, after a long silence, someone in the audience asked a question. And I—it—spoke. It was called upon for a response, and its answer met the question. Nobody needed the response; I had nothing to say that people didn't already know in themselves. Yet the response happened. It was necessary. How do I know it was necessary? Because it happened.

The reason this speaks is because it does. If I thought I was doing it, I wouldn't be such a fool. My only purpose is to do what I'm apparently doing. When I do The Work with someone, my purpose is to sit with that person and ask the questions. If someone asks me a question, my purpose is to give my experience through my answer. I'm an effect of their suffering; there's no cause arising here. The cause is what people would call outside me, and their outside is my inside. When someone talks, I'm a listener. When someone asks, I'm a response.

I understand spiritual teachers who are silent, and this one speaks. It had to go all the way. It had to take all the risks. It wouldn't let any concept of "I shouldn't say anything at all because no words are true" stop it. It says "you and I," and that's where the scam begins.

Just after my experience at the halfway house in 1986, it was difficult for me to say anything. *Table* was a lie. *Bird* was a lie. *Tree* was a lie. Every word separated the world into parts and seemed to teach what didn't exist. I couldn't say the word *I* without feeling a loss of integrity. Eventually, I found a way of speaking that seemed less untrue. Instead of "I want a glass of water," I would say, "She thinks she wants a glass of water now"; instead of "I'm hungry," I would say, "It thinks it's hungry now." That was as close as I could get to integrity and still be able to communicate. Later, when the communication became more mature, I began to say, "I'm hungry" or "I want a glass of water." This seemed like an incredible act of deceit and courage at the same time. I felt as if, through language, I would be teaching a lie and become lost in the non-existent again. But I used the *I* because I wanted to join with other people. It was a way of giving myself to them. I surrendered into that language out of love. I will still sometimes refer to myself as *she* or *we* or *you*. I will take on any pronoun, and sometimes it's hard for people to grasp that. I can't see any separation as real.

So it originally appeared as a liar—for love. It would do anything for love, it would say anything. It would die for it, over and over and over. It would sell its peace, if that were possible. It has no caring for itself. It dies for itself; it lives for itself. It will internally join anyone and anything. It will join because it *is* the other already.

Because it is not attached to words or things, it is free to give you everything it has, everything it is. Everything in the world is like this, constantly giving itself, constantly pouring itself out into the world, *as* the world. Generosity is our very nature, and when we try to pretend otherwise, when we hold back or give with a motive, it hurts. A motive is just an unquestioned thought. On the other side of our thinking, generosity naturally appears. There's nothing we need to do to achieve it. It's simply what we are.

How to Do The Work

(adapted from *Loving What Is* and www.thework.com)

The one criticism of The Work I consistently hear is that it's just too simple. People say, "Freedom can't be this simple!" I answer, "Can you really know that that's true?"

Judge your neighbor, write it down, ask four questions, turn it around. Who says that freedom has to be complicated?

PUTTING THE MIND ON PAPER

The first step in The Work is to write down your judgments about any stressful situation in your life—past, present, or future—about a person you dislike or worry about, a situation with someone who angers or frightens or saddens you, or someone you're ambivalent or confused about. Write your judgments down, just the way you think them. Write in short, simple sentences. (Use a blank sheet of paper; or go to www.thework.com, to the Downloads section of the Resources tab, where you'll find a Judge-Your-Neighbor Worksheet to download and print.)

For thousands of years we have been taught not to judge—but let's face it, we still do it all the time. The truth is that we all have judgments running in our heads. Through The Work we finally have permission to let those judgments speak out, or even scream out, on paper. We may find that even the most unpleasant thoughts can be met with unconditional love.

I encourage you to write about someone whom you haven't yet totally forgiven. This is the most powerful place to begin. Even if you've forgiven that person 99 percent, you aren't free until your forgiveness is complete. The 1 percent you haven't forgiven them is the very place where you're stuck in all your other relationships (including your relationship with yourself).

If you are new to inquiry, I strongly suggest that you not write about yourself at first. When you start by judging yourself, your answers come with a motive and with solutions that haven't worked. Judging someone else, then inquiring and turning it around, is the direct path to understanding. You can judge yourself later, when you have been doing inquiry long enough to trust the power of truth.

If you begin by pointing the finger of blame outward, then the focus isn't on you. You can just let loose and be uncensored. We're often quite sure about what other people need to do, how they should live, whom they should be with. We have 20/20 vision about other people, but not about ourselves.

When you do The Work, you see who you are by seeing who you think other people are. Eventually you come to see that everything outside you is a reflection of your own thinking. You are the storyteller, the projector of all stories, and the world is the projected image of your thoughts.

Since the beginning of time, people have been trying to change the world so that they can be happy. This hasn't ever worked, because it approaches the problem backward. What The Work gives us is a way to change the projector—mind—rather than the projected. It's like when there's a piece of lint on a projector's lens. We think there's a flaw on the screen, and we try to change this person and that person, whomever the flaw appears to be on next. But it's futile to try to change the projected images. Once we realize where the lint is, we can clear the lens itself. This is the end of suffering, and the beginning of a little joy in paradise.

How to Write on the Worksheet

Please avoid the temptation to continue without writing down your judgments. If you try to do The Work in your head, without putting your thoughts on paper, the mind will outsmart you. Before you're even aware of it, it will be off and running into another story to prove that it's right. But though the mind can justify itself faster than the speed of light, it can be stopped through the act of writing. Once the mind is stopped on paper, thoughts remain stable, and inquiry can easily be applied.

I invite you to be judgmental, harsh, childish, and petty. Write with the spontaneity of a child who is sad, angry, confused, or frightened. Don't try to be wise, spiritual, or kind. This is the time to be totally honest and uncensored about how you feel. Allow your feelings to express themselves, without any fear of consequences or any threat of punishment. Be sure to write in short, simple sentences.

Write down the thoughts and stories that are running through you, the ones that really cause you pain—the anger, the resentment, the sadness. Point the finger of blame first at people who have hurt you, the ones who have been closest to you, people you're jealous of, people you can't stand, people who have disappointed you. "My husband left me." "My partner infected me with AIDS." "My mother didn't love me." "My children don't respect me." "My friend betrayed me." "I hate my boss." "I hate my neighbors; they're ruining my life." Write about what you read this morning in the newspaper, about people being murdered or losing their homes through famine or war. Write about the checker at the grocery store who was too slow or about the driver who cut you off on the freeway. Every story is a variation on a single theme: *This shouldn't be happening. I shouldn't have to experience this. God is unjust. Life isn't fair.*

People new to The Work sometimes think, "I don't know what to write. Why should I do The Work anyway? I'm not angry at anyone. Nothing's really bothering me." If you don't know what to write about, wait. Life will give you a topic. Maybe a friend didn't call you back when she said she would, and you're disappointed. Maybe when you were five years old, your mother punished you for something you didn't do. Maybe you're upset or frightened when you read the newspaper or think about the suffering in the world.

Put on paper the part of your mind that is saying these things. You can't stop the story inside your head, however hard you try. It's not possible. But when you put the story on paper and write it just the way the mind is telling it, with all your suffering and frustration and rage and sadness, then you can take a look at what's swirling around inside you. You can see it brought into the material world, in physical form. And, finally, through The Work, you can begin to understand it.

When a child gets lost, he may feel sheer terror. It can be just as frightening when you're lost inside the mind's chaos. But when you enter The Work, it is possible to find order and to learn the way back home. It doesn't matter what street you walk down, there's something familiar; you know where you are. You could be kidnapped and someone hides you away for a month and then throws you blindfolded out of a car, but when you take off the blindfold and look at the buildings and streets, you begin to recognize a phone booth or a grocery store, and everything becomes familiar. You know what to do to find your way home. That is how The Work functions. Once the mind is met with understanding, it can always find its way back home. There is no place where you can remain lost or confused.

THE JUDGE-YOUR-NEIGHBOR WORKSHEET

After my life changed in 1986, I spent a lot of time in the desert near my home, just listening to myself. Stories arose inside me that had been troubling mankind forever. Sooner or later I witnessed every concept, it seemed, and I discovered that even though I was alone in the desert, the whole world was with me. And it sounded like this: "I want," "I need," "they should," "they shouldn't," "I'm angry because," "I'm sad," "I'll never," "I don't want to." These phrases, which repeated themselves over and over in my mind, became the basis for the Judge-Your-Neighbor Worksheet. The purpose of the Worksheet is to help you put your painful stories and judgments into writing; it's designed to draw out judgments that otherwise might be difficult to uncover.

The judgments you write on the Worksheet will become the material that you'll use to do The Work. You'll put each written statement—one by one—up against the four questions and let each of them lead you to the truth.

Here is an example of a completed Judge-Your-Neighbor Worksheet. I have written about my second husband, Paul, in this example (included here with his permission); these are the kinds of thoughts that I used to have about him before my life changed. As you read, you're invited to replace Paul's name with the name of the appropriate person in your life.

1. Who angers, confuses, saddens, or disappoints you, and why? What is it about them that you don't like?

    I am angry at Paul because he doesn't appreciate me. I'm angry at Paul because he doesn't listen to me. I don't like Paul because he argues with everything I say.

2. How do you want them to change? What do you want them to do?

    I want Paul to give me his full attention. I want Paul to love me completely. I want Paul to stop arguing with everything I say. I want Paul to agree with me. I want Paul to get more exercise.

3. What is it that they should or shouldn't do, be, think, or feel? What advice could you offer?

    Paul shouldn't watch so much television. Paul should stop smoking. Paul should tell me that he loves me. He shouldn't ignore what I say.

4. Do you need anything from them? What do they need to do in order for you to be happy?

    I need Paul to listen to me. I need Paul to stop lying to me. I need Paul to share his feelings and be emotionally available. I need Paul to be gentle and kind and patient.

5. What do you think of them? Make a list. (Remember, be petty and judgmental.)

Paul is dishonest. Paul is reckless. Paul is dangerous to my children's security and welfare. He thinks he doesn't have to follow the rules. Paul is uncaring and unavailable. Paul is irresponsible. Paul should stop gambling and lying about money.

6. What is it that you don't want to experience with that person again?

I don't ever want to live with Paul if he doesn't change. I don't ever want to argue with Paul again. I don't ever want to be lied to by Paul again. I don't ever want to worry about what credit cards are hidden from me or what checks are written without my knowledge.

INQUIRY: THE FOUR QUESTIONS AND TURNAROUND

1. **Is it true?**
2. **Can you absolutely know that it's true?**
3. **How do you react when you believe that thought?**
4. **Who would you be without the thought?**
   and

Turn it around.

Now, using the four questions, let's investigate part of the first statement from number 1 on the example: *Paul doesn't appreciate me.* As you read along, think of someone you have had the same belief about.

1. **Is it true?** Ask yourself, "Is it true that Paul doesn't appreciate me?" Be still. If you really want to know the truth, the answer will rise to meet the question. Let the mind ask the question, and wait for the answer to surface.

Reality, for me, is what is true. The truth is whatever is in front of you, whatever is really happening. Whether you like it or not, it's raining now. "It shouldn't be raining" is just a thought. In reality, there is no such thing as a "should" or a "shouldn't." These are only thoughts that we impose onto reality. Without the "should" and "shouldn't," we can see reality as it is, and this leaves us free to act efficiently, clearly, and sanely.

When asking the first question, take your time. The Work is about discovering what is true from the deepest part of yourself. You are listening for *your* answers now, not other people's, and not anything you have been taught. This can be very unsettling, because you're entering the unknown. As you continue to dive deeper, allow the truth within you to rise and meet the question. Be gentle as you give yourself to inquiry. Let this experience have you completely.

2. **Can you absolutely know that it's true?** If your answer to question 1 was no, then move on to question 3. If your answer was yes, ask yourself, "Can I absolutely know that it's true?" In many cases, the statement appears to be true. Of course it does. Your concepts are based on a lifetime of uninvestigated beliefs. Consider these questions: "Can I absolutely know that it's true that Paul doesn't appreciate me? Can I ever really know when someone is appreciating me or not? Am I sometimes appreciating someone even when I don't express it?"

After I woke up to reality in 1986, I noticed many times how people, in conversations, the media, and books, made statements such as "There isn't enough understanding in the world," "There's too much violence," "We should love one another more." These were stories I used to believe, too. They seemed sensitive, kind, and caring, but as I heard them, I noticed that believing them caused stress and that they didn't feel peaceful inside me.

For instance, when I heard the story "People should be more loving," the question would arise in me "Can I absolutely know that that's true? Can I really know for myself, within myself, that people should be more loving? Even if the whole world tells me so, is it really true?" And, to my amazement, when I listened within myself, I saw that the world is what it is—nothing more, nothing less. Where reality is concerned, there is no "what should be." There is only what is, just the way it is, right now. The truth is prior to every story. And every story, prior to investigation, prevents us from seeing what's true.

Now I could finally inquire of every potentially uncomfortable story, "Can I absolutely know that it's true?" And the answer, like the question, was an experience: No. I would stand rooted in that answer—solitary, peaceful, free.

How could no be the right answer? Everyone I knew, and all the books, said that the answer should be yes. But I came to see that the truth is itself and will not be dictated to by anyone. In the presence of that inner no, I came to see that the world is always as it should be, whether I opposed it or not. And I came to embrace reality with all my heart. I love the world, without any conditions.

If your answer is still yes, good. If you think that you can absolutely know that that's true, it's always fine to move on to question 3.

3. **How do you react when you believe that thought?** With this question, we begin to notice internal cause and effect. You can see that when you believe the thought, there is an uneasy feeling, a disturbance that can range from mild discomfort to fear or panic.

How do you react when you believe that Paul doesn't appreciate you? Now, with your eyes closed, watch how you treat him when you believe that thought. Make a list. For example: "I give him 'the look.' I interrupt him. I punish him by not paying attention to him. I sulk, I withdraw, I stop appreciating him and become resentful of all the kind things that I have done for him." Continue making your list as you go inside, and see how you treat yourself in that situation and how that feels. "I imagine leaving him and imagine how much better my life would be without him, how he will be sorry when I'm gone, how no one will appreciate him as much as I do. I am taken over by self-pity. I shut down. I isolate myself. I eat and sleep a lot, and I watch television for days. I feel depressed and lonely." Notice all the effects of believing the thought "Paul doesn't appreciate me." Notice where the thought hits you in your body. Close your eyes and track it; see how much of your body the thought takes over.

After the four questions found me, I would notice thoughts like

"People should be more loving," and I would see that they caused a feeling of uneasiness. I noticed that prior to the thought, there was peace. My mind was quiet and serene. This is who I am without my story. Then, in the stillness of awareness, I began to notice the feelings that came from believing or attaching to the thought. And in the stillness I could see that if I were to believe the thought, the result would be a feeling of unease and sadness. When I asked, "How do I react when I believe the thought that people should be more loving?" I saw that not only did I have an uncomfortable feeling (this was obvious), but I also reacted with mental pictures to prove that the thought was true. I flew off into a world that didn't exist. I reacted by living in a stressed body, seeing everything through fearful eyes, a sleepwalker, someone in an endless nightmare. The remedy was simply to investigate.

I love question 3. Once you answer it for yourself, once you see the cause and effect of a thought, all your suffering begins to unravel.

4. **Who would you be without the thought?** This is a very powerful question. Picture yourself standing in the presence of the person you have written about when they're doing what you think they should or shouldn't be doing. Consider, for example, who you would be without the thought "Paul doesn't appreciate me." Who would you be if you weren't even capable of thinking that thought? Close your eyes and imagine Paul not appreciating you. Imagine you don't have the thought that Paul doesn't appreciate you (or that he even *should* appreciate you). Take your time. Notice what is revealed to you. What do you see? How does that feel?

For many people, life without their story is literally unimaginable. They have no reference for it. So "I don't know" is a common answer to this question. Other people answer by saying, "I'd be free," "I'd be peaceful," "I'd be a more loving person." You could also say, "I'd be clear enough to understand the situation and act efficiently." Without our stories, we are not only able to act clearly, kindly, and fearlessly; we are also a friend, a listener. We are people living happy lives. We are appreciation and gratitude that have become as natural as breath itself. Happiness is the natural state for someone who knows that there's nothing to know and that we already have everything we need, right here, now.

Turn it around. To do the turnaround, rewrite your statement. First, write it as if it were written about you. Where you have written someone's name, put yourself. Instead of "he" or "she," put "I." For example, "Paul doesn't appreciate me" turns around to "I don't appreciate Paul" and "I don't appreciate myself." Another type is a 180-degree turnaround to the extreme opposite: "Paul does appreciate me." For each turnaround, find three genuine examples of how the turnaround is true in your life. This is not about blaming yourself or feeling guilty. It's about discovering alternatives that can bring you peace.

The turnaround is a very powerful part of The Work. As long as you think that the cause of your problem is "out there"—as long as you think that anyone or anything else is responsible for your suffering—the situation is hopeless. It means that you are forever in the role of the victim, that you're suffering in paradise. So bring the truth home to yourself and begin to set yourself free. Inquiry combined with the turnaround is the fast track to self-realization.

THE TURNAROUND FOR NUMBER 6

The turnaround for statement number 6 on the Judge-Your-Neighbor Worksheet is a bit different from the others. We change "I don't ever want to . . ." to "I am willing to . . ." and "I look forward to . . ." For example, "I don't ever want to argue with Paul again" turns around to "I am willing to argue with Paul again" and "I look forward to arguing with Paul again." Why would you look forward to it? This turnaround is about fully embracing all of mind and life without fear, and being open to reality. It's about welcoming all your thoughts and experiences with open arms. If you experience an argument with Paul again, good. If it hurts, you can put your thoughts on paper and investigate them. Uncomfortable feelings are merely the reminders that we've attached to something that may not be true for us. They let us know that it's time to do The Work.

If you feel any resistance to a thought, your Work is not done. When you can honestly look forward to experiences that have been uncomfortable, there is no longer anything to fear in life; you see everything as a gift that can bring you self-realization.

It's good to acknowledge that the same feelings or situation may happen again, if only in your thoughts. When you realize that suffering and discomfort are the call to inquiry, you may actually begin to look forward to uncomfortable feelings. You may even experience them as friends coming to show you what you have not yet investigated thoroughly enough. It's no longer necessary to wait for people or situations to change in order to experience peace and harmony. The Work is the direct way to orchestrate your own happiness.

After sitting with the turnarounds, you would continue a typical inquiry with the next statement written in number 1 on the Worksheet—*Paul doesn't listen to me*—and then with every other statement on the Worksheet. For further instructions, read *Loving What Is* or visit www.thework.com.

YOUR TURN: THE WORKSHEET

Now you know enough to try out The Work. First you'll put your thoughts on paper. Fill in the blanks below, writing about someone you haven't yet forgiven 100 percent. Remember to *point the finger of blame or judgment outward.* You may write from your present position or from your point of view as a five-year-old or a twenty-five-year-old. Do not write about yourself yet. Use short, simple sentences. Please don't censor yourself—allow yourself to be as judgmental and petty as you really feel. Don't try to be "spiritual" or kind.

1. Who angers, confuses, saddens, or disappoints you, and why? What is it about them that you don't like? (Remember: Be harsh, childish, and petty.)

I don't like (I am angry at, or saddened, frustrated, frightened, confused, etc., by) [*name*] because _____

_____.

2. How do you want them to change? What do you want them to do?

I want [*name*] to_____

_____.

3. What is it that they should or shouldn't do, be, think, or feel? What advice could you offer?

[*Name*] should (shouldn't) _____

_____.

4. Do you need anything from them? What do they need to do in order for you to be happy? (Pretend it's your birthday and you can have anything you want. Go for it!)

I need [*name*] to _____

_____.

5. What do you think of them? Make a list. (Don't be rational or kind.)

[*Name*] is _____

_____.

6. What is it that you don't want to experience with that person again?

I don't ever want _____

_____.

YOUR TURN: THE INQUIRY

One by one, put each statement on the Judge-Your-Neighbor Worksheet up against the four questions, then turn around the statement you're working on and find three genuine examples of how each turnaround is true. (If you need help, refer back to the example.) Throughout this process, explore being open to possibilities beyond what you think you know. There's nothing more exciting than discovering the don't-know mind.

It's like diving. Keep asking the question and wait. Let the answer find you. You may begin to experience revelations about yourself and your world, revelations that can transform your whole life, forever.

Questions and Answers

Q   *I have a hard time writing about others. Can I write about myself?*

A   If you want to know yourself, I suggest you write about someone else. Point The Work outward in the beginning, and you may come to see that everything outside you is a direct reflection of your own thinking. It's all about you. Most of us have been pointing our criticism and judgments at ourselves for years, and it hasn't solved anything yet. Judging someone else, inquiring, and turning it around is the fast path to understanding and self-realization.

Q   *Do I have to write? Can't I just ask the questions and turn it around in my head when I have a problem?*

A   Mind's job is to be right, and it can justify itself faster than the speed of light. Stop the portion of your thinking that is the source of your fear, anger, sadness, or resentment by transferring it to paper. Once the mind is stopped on paper, it's much easier to investigate. Eventually The Work begins to undo you automatically, even without writing.

Q   *What if I don't have a problem with people? Can I write about* things, *like my body?*

A   Yes. Do The Work on any subject that is stressful. As you become familiar with the four questions and the turnaround, you may choose subjects such as the body, disease, career, or even God. Then experiment with using the term "my thinking" in place of the subject when you do the turnarounds.

Example: "My body should be flexible and healthy" becomes "My thinking should be flexible and healthy." Isn't that what you really want—a balanced, healthy mind? Has a sick body ever been a problem, or is it your thinking about the body that causes the problem? Investigate. Let your doctor take care of your body as you take care of your thinking. Freedom doesn't require a healthy body. Free your mind, and the body will follow.

Q *I've heard you say that you're a lover of reality. What about war, rape, poverty, violence, and child abuse? Are you condoning them?*

A Quite the opposite. How could I condone anything that isn't kind? I simply notice that if I believe they shouldn't exist when they do exist, I suffer. Can I just end the war in me? Can I stop raping myself and others with my abusive thoughts and actions? If not, I'm continuing in myself the very thing I want to end in the world. I start with ending my own suffering, my own war. This is a life's work.

Q *So what you're saying is that I should just accept reality as it is and not argue with it. Is that right?*

A The Work doesn't say what anyone should or shouldn't do. We simply ask, "What is the effect of arguing with reality? How does it feel?" This Work explores the cause and effect of attaching to painful thoughts, and in that investigation we find our freedom. To simply say that we shouldn't argue with reality just adds another story, another philosophy or religion. It hasn't ever worked.

Q *Loving what is sounds like never wanting anything. Isn't it more interesting to want things?*

A My experience is that I do want something all the time: What I want is what is. It's not only interesting, it's ecstatic! When I want what I have, thought and action aren't separate; they move as one, without conflict. If you find anything lacking, ever, write down your thoughts and question them all the way through. I find that life never falls short and doesn't require a future. Everything I need is always supplied, and I don't have to do anything for it. There is nothing more exciting than loving what is.

Q   *Is inquiry a process of thinking? If not, what is it?*
A   Inquiry appears to be a process of thinking, but actually it's a way to undo thinking. Thoughts lose their power over us when we realize that they simply appear in the mind. They're not personal. Through The Work, instead of escaping or suppressing our thoughts, we learn to meet them with open arms.

Q   *I don't believe in God. Can I still benefit from The Work?*
A   Yes. Atheist, agnostic, Christian, Jew, Muslim, Buddhist, Hindu, pagan—we all have one thing in common: We want happiness and peace. If you are tired of suffering, I invite you to The Work.

Q   *Is there a way I can go deeper with The Work?*
A   I often say, "If you really want to be free, have The Work for breakfast." The more you do inquiry, the more it undoes you. Some people prefer to do The Work as part of an organized program, so I offer the nine-day School for The Work, an intense and life-changing journey through your own mind. You can read more about the School at www.thework.com.

Q   *I understand the process of inquiry intellectually, but I don't really feel anything shifting when I do it. What am I missing?*
A   If you answer the questions superficially with the thinking mind, the process will leave you feeling disconnected. Try asking the question and going deeper. You may have to ask the question a few times to stay focused, but as you practice this, an answer will slowly arise. When the answer comes from inside you, the realizations and shifts follow naturally.

Q   *I've been using the turnarounds whenever I make judgments, and somehow it doesn't do anything but make me depressed and confused. What's going on?*

A To simply turn thoughts around keeps the process intellectual and is of little value. The invitation is to go beyond the intellect. The questions are like probes that dive into the mind, bringing deeper knowledge to the surface. Ask the questions first, and then wait. Once the answers have arisen, the superficial mind and the deeper mind meet, and the turnarounds feel like true discoveries.

ACKNOWLEDGMENTS

I would like to acknowledge Adam Joseph Lewis for his unwavering love and generosity in making The Work available to so many people throughout the world.

I would also like to express my deep gratitude to Michael Katz, my agent, and Josh Baran, my publicist, for their help in the shaping of this book; to Dr. David A. Soskis and to Carol Williams, who each gave the manuscript a meticulous reading and offered many suggestions for improvement; to Michele Penner, Ellen Mack, and Prem Rikta, who collected and edited some older selections that were spliced in here and there; to Bill Birdsall, Lisa Biskup, Paula Brittain, Melony Malouf, Mischelle Miller, and Lesley Pollitt; and to the many thousands of people who have moved The Work in the name of peace.

ABOUT THE AUTHORS

BYRON KATIE discovered inquiry in 1986. She has been traveling around the world for more than a dozen years, teaching The Work directly to hundreds of thousands of people at free public events, in prisons, hospitals, churches, corporations, battered women's facilities, universities and schools, at weekend intensives, and at her nine-day School for The Work. (A few years ago a friend traveling in India e-mailed that he shared a train compartment with two young German women who were happily doing Katie's Work together as the train rolled through the mangrove swamps. They had been introduced to it at a workshop in Denmark.) She is the author of two bestselling books: *Loving What Is* and *I Need Your Love—Is That True?* Her website is www.thework.com.

STEPHEN MITCHELL's many books include the bestselling *Tao Te Ching, The Gospel According to Jesus, Bhagavad Gita, The Book of Job, Meetings with the Archangel,* and *Gilgamesh.* You can read extensive excerpts from all his books on his website, www.stephenmitchellbooks.com.

Visit www.thework.com and change your life.

- Learn more about The Work

- Download audio and video clips of Byron Katie doing The Work with others

- Print out Worksheets for daily use

- Establish a daily practice on the NetWork, find a facilitator, call the free hotline

- See Katie's schedule of events

- Join Katie's Parlor

- Find out about the nine-day School for The Work with Byron Katie

- Visit the store for Katie's books, CDs, and DVDs

ALSO BY BYRON KATIE

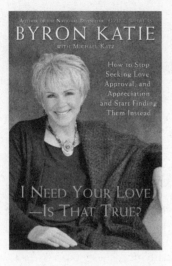
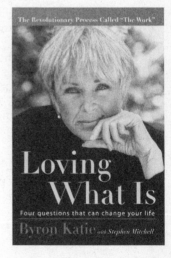